"A powerful book about the importance of friendships, belonging, and human connection that helps us infuse every relationship with more meaning and purpose. We need *Friendship in the Age of Loneliness* now more than ever."

—CASSIDY BLACKWELL, DIRECTOR OF
INTERNATIONAL COMMUNICATIONS AT AIRBNB

"A practical guide to fostering human connection and true friendship in an increasingly lonely, isolated, digital world."

—DAN SCHAWBEL, *WASHINGTON POST*
BESTSELLING AUTHOR OF *BACK TO HUMAN*

"Smiley's writing is authentic, heart-centered, and powerful. A must-read for HR leaders, company culture pioneers, and anyone who cares about their people. Simply put, this book is exactly what the world needs right now."

—CLAUDE SILVER, CHIEF HEART OFFICER AT VAYNERMEDIA

"*Friendship in the Age of Loneliness* is an essential call to find belonging—with yourself, with your friends, with your co-workers, and in your communities. We all need this book."

—DAVID SPINKS, COFOUNDER OF CMX AND
AUTHOR OF *THE BUSINESS OF BELONGING*

an

optimist's guide

to connection

# Friendship

in the age of

# Loneliness

adam smiley

poswolsky

RUNNING PRESS

PHILADELPHIA

Running Press
Hachette Book Group
1290 Avenue of the Americas, New York, NY 10104
www.runningpress.com
@Running_Press

Printed in the United States of America

First Edition: May 2021

Published by Running Press, an imprint of Perseus Books, LLC,
a subsidiary of Hachette Book Group, Inc. The Running Press name
and logo is a trademark of the Hachette Book Group.

The publisher is not responsible for websites (or their content) that
are not owned by the publisher.

Cover design by Samantha Russo, interior design by Joanna Price.

Library of Congress Control Number: 2020947764

ISBNs: 978-0-7624-7227-7 (hardcover), 978-0-7624-7226-0 (ebook),
978-1-5491-3332-9 (audio book)

LSC-C

Printing 1, 2021

*For anyone who has ever lost
a friend or felt like they didn't
have a friend to talk to.*

———

*For Levi. I miss you. We miss you.
Planet Earth misses you.*

# Contents

# The Power of Friendship in a Pandemic

Friendship sustains us through the most trying of times. As I was writing this book, the COVID-19 virus swept across the world, killing hundreds of thousands of people, putting millions out of work, and forever changing the way we gather. Suddenly, so many of the things we take for granted—like meeting up with a friend at a coffee shop, visiting a family member, going to the gym, or even shaking someone's hand—became forbidden activities.

While the pandemic threatened to make us even more lonely, it also gave us a window into what's possible when we come together and put our shared humanity first. We raised money for PPE for nurses and doctors; sewed masks for friends and family members; cooked food for essential workers; fund-raised to keep our favorite restaurants, independent bookshops, and music venues open; and delivered groceries to the elderly.

Three restaurant employees started the Service Workers Coalition, raising more than eighty thousand dollars for sick or quarantined workers in New York City. The Minnestota COVIDSitters, with their tagline "Caring for your family while you care for ours," matched hundreds of volunteers with hospital workers—including custodians, cooks, and other essential employees—in need of help babysitting, pet-sitting, and running errands. Every night at seven o'clock, entire neighborhoods erupted in cheers to honor, celebrate, and thank hospital staff and frontline workers.

With social distancing regulations in place, people had to get creative in order to spend time with each other. Inspired by videos coming out of Italy, people sang with each other from their apartment balconies and front stoops. Quarantined Berklee College of Music students gave a virtual performance of "What the World Needs Now Is Love," which was viewed more than two million times on YouTube.

In Bernal Heights, my partner's neighborhood in San Francisco and where I spent much of the lockdown, a small newspaper was created for children, bookshelves became sidewalk food banks, and garages turned into medical-supply distribution centers. There were socially distanced dance parties, elaborate garden scavenger hunts for kids, a pop-up bakery, and stoop cocktail parties.

To surprise my friend Seth on his birthday, ten of us showed up outside his house in Oakland wearing pictures of Seth's face on our masks and danced the Macarena while staying six feet apart from each other. We each recorded a birthday video message for Seth that his brother, Zev, edited into a forty-five-minute montage, complete with a soundtrack and childhood home videos.

For their three-year-old son's birthday party, my friends invited folks to drive by their house and honk their horns; even the local fire department showed up with their sirens on and lights flashing to celebrate.

"Being forced into isolation has made it abundantly clear how much we mean to each other, and how much we need each other," observed Kat Vellos, friendship expert and author of *We Should Get Together*. "People are reaching out and offering support to each other in ways that would never have just spontaneously happened while everyone was rushing around living their normal lives. What is emerging now are: openness, generosity, slowing down, valuing each other, and valuing life."

Friends offered each other free virtual art classes, cooking lessons, and career coaching. Some began reading each other bedtime poems and stories over FaceTime. Others did Morning Pages together, opening a video chat to write in their journals at the same time each morning. Others hosted "artifact shares," where they gathered with a group of friends on a Zoom video and shared a piece of the place where they spent their time during quarantine. There were Zoom happy hours, musical performances streamed on Facebook Live, DJs who had been booked to play at Coachella playing on Instagram live instead, dance parties on Twitch, Netflix parties, WhatsApp group threads to share recipes, MarcoPolo chats to share fun video messages, office hours for strangers, and dinner parties where friends would order the same take-out meal from their favorite restaurant and eat "together" over video chat.

Prior to coronavirus, my best friends from college and I would only get to see each other once every two years, usually at a bachelor party or a wedding. But starting the first week of quarantine, we would have a Zoom call every Wednesday evening to check in and support our buddy Gabe, an emergency room doctor working at Mount Sinai Hospital and Elmhurst Hospital in New York. We kept meeting up weekly—for three months straight. Instead of having a Sunday check-in call once a week, my family started FaceTiming four times a week so I could see my parents, my sister, and my nine-month-old nephew on video three thousand miles away.

On Passover, my partner and I got to attend three different Passover Seders, with my family in Boston, her dad's family in Florida, and her mom's family in New York, all without leaving our couch in San Francisco. The thought of Jewish families *kvetching* at each other all around the world, trying to figure out how to set up their Zoom Seders, saying, "Can you see my Haggadah?!" and "Just press gallery view!" over and over again filled me with joy.

The pandemic demonstrated the true power of friendship to sustain us through everything life throws at us. We bore witness to why human interaction is essential to our health and well-being. During quarantine, I often heard people say, "I see more of my friends' faces now than before quarantine. We really should have these reunions more often when non-Zoom life resumes."

There was a refreshing sensation that technology was being used intentionally for one of its original and most noble purposes: to spark human connection and facilitate belonging. Sherry Turkle, Abby Rockefeller Mauzé Professor of the Social Studies of Science and Technology at MIT, wrote in *Politico*, "This is a different life on the screen from disappearing into a video game or polishing one's avatar. This is breaking open a medium with human generosity and empathy. This is looking within and asking: 'What can I authentically offer? I have a life, a history. What do people need?' If, moving forward, we apply our most human instincts to our devices, that will have been a powerful COVID-19 legacy. Not only alone together, but together alone."

Contrary to expectations that COVID-19 would make us even lonelier, a comprehensive study published in the journal *American Psychologist* actually found that social distancing protocols and stay-at-home orders *did not* lead to an increase in loneliness among Americans. Researchers found resilience, not loneliness, in their nationwide research. "Contrary to this fear, we found that overall loneliness did not increase," said Martina Luchetti, an assistant professor at the Florida State University College of Medicine and lead author of the study. "Instead, people felt more supported by others than before the pandemic. Even while physically isolated, the feeling of increased social support and of being in this together may help limit increases in loneliness."

The legacy of COVID-19 will certainly include an incalculable loss of human life, a strain on public health, widespread economic hardship, and an awakening to the deep structural inequalities in our society. However, I'm hopeful that this time will also serve as a reminder of what matters most: our interconnectedness. That we can't afford to take our people or our planet for granted. That our existence is not guaranteed. That we won't survive without looking out for one another.

That we will approach our lives less from a place of "Ugh! *I have to* go to work, school, or a friend's birthday party," and more from, "Wow! *I get to* go to work, school, or a friend's birthday party." That we will celebrate our shared humanity and cherish the simple yet profound freedom to congregate in public, to go see live music, to sit inside a restaurant, to visit family, to hug an old friend, to pass countless hours with our people, and realize just how lucky we are to be alive together.

# The Revolutionary Act of Connection in the Digital Age

Not long ago, I went through a rough period of loneliness and sadness. This might come as a surprise to some, since my nickname is Smiley, and I have 4,867 Facebook friends. My social media depicts this life of a successful author who travels around the world speaking and helping people figure out their purpose. I bump into people, and the first thing they say to me, without even asking how I am, is, "Smiley, you're killing it! Your life is dope."

I really want to tell them that I'm lonely. That I'm constantly comparing myself to others. That I'm tired of traveling. That I miss my real friends. That despite how good everything looks online, my real life feels very different. I often feel sad, overwhelmed, exhausted, burned out, and alone.

I thought to myself, "If I'm feeling this way, then other people probably are, too."

The more I talked to people in my community, the more I realized they were struggling with the same things. In fact, the people who seemed to be the most "popular" or "connected" or "successful" in terms of their online presence and their "brand" were actually the people struggling the most with loneliness and knowing who their true friends were. In my interviews with hundreds of millennials about their friendships, I found that there was a direct correlation between the number of Facebook friends or Instagram followers someone had and the *lack* of deep friendships they felt they actually had in their life.

I kept hearing things like:

"I spend all this time interacting with people online, but I don't feel like I have someone to turn to when I'm struggling."

"My Instagram life is a lot prettier than my actual life."

"I go to a lot of events, I'm part of many different communities— but I feel like I don't really know most of those people well. I keep seeing all these people in large groups but never in an intimate setting. When I try to make one-on-one plans, people say they're busy or they flake out."

"I'm tired of meeting new people; I want to go deeper with the friends I already have."

"It's been a long time since I spent a whole day just relaxing with a friend."

Something was up: not only were people lying online about how happy they were (F you, social media!), but perhaps more alarmingly, *they had lost track of how to show up for their actual friends*—the thing most likely to make them happier in the first place.

This mirrors dozens of studies showing that adults are feeling lonelier than ever, with fewer friendships at work and outside of work. In their 2013 *State of Friendship in America* report, the social research organization Lifeboat found that the average American adult only has one real friend and that three-quarters of Americans are not satisfied with their friendships. In 2019, Evite reported that the average American hasn't made a new friend in the last five years.

We might be messaging with our "friends" for hours online, but we don't know who to call when we actually need a friend to talk with. Lifeboat discovered that one in four Americans say they don't have someone to turn to for meaningful conversation (including family members), and the BBC reported that 200,000 people haven't spoken to a close relative in over a month.

In a 55,000-person BBC survey in 2018, the world's largest loneliness study, 40 percent of sixteen- to twenty-four-year-olds reported feeling lonely *often* or *very often*. The problem is only getting worse: in a national Cigna survey of 10,000 US adults in 2019, *three in five* Americans (61 percent) reported feeling lonely (up from 54 percent in 2018), and younger generations were lonelier than older generations. Nearly 80 percent of Gen-Zers and 70 percent of millennials are lonely.

As friendships are dwindling, social media use is flourishing, especially among young people: according to the Pew Research Center, 90 percent of eighteen- to twenty-nine-year-olds regularly use social media, and 45 percent of teens aged thirteen to seventeen use the internet "almost constantly." TikTok—the number one downloaded app of 2020—has more than eight hundred million monthly active users, with 70 percent being under the age of twenty-four, and 30 percent being thirteen to seventeen years old. Social media addiction becomes even more alarming, considering research that has linked rising rates of teen mental health challenges, including depression and suicide, to increased smartphone and social media use. The suicide rate for young people aged ten to twenty-four increased by 56 percent between 2007 and 2017 (for children aged ten to fourteen, it tripled), according to the CDC.

Jane Brody, personal health columnist for the *New York Times*, reminds us that people can be socially isolated and not feel lonely, and, likewise, people can feel lonely even when they have lots of social connections, especially if those relationships are not emotionally rewarding. In other words, social isolation and loneliness are different. According to psychologists Julianne Holt-Lunstad and Timothy B. Smith, "Social isolation denotes having few connections or interactions, whereas loneliness involves the subjective perception of isolation—the discrepancy between one's desired and actual level of connection."

In response to these mounting pressures of modern life, we've been prescribed every potential cure under the sun: Quit social media, download a meditation app, declutter your house, become indistractable, subtly not give a fu*k, be a badass, use a bullet journal, go paleo, go keto, get a Peloton, do CrossFit, *do nothing*—the list goes on.

Yet we rarely talk about the simple power of spending more time with friends. We tap our phones 2,600 times a day and look at our phone every twelve minutes, and spend fifty minutes a day on Facebook and Instagram; yet we spend just 4 percent *(4 percent!)* of our time with friends.

As journalist Johann Hari's research on depression has shown, we need to talk much more about social recovery. "If you have a crisis in your life, you'll notice something: it won't be your Twitter followers who come to sit with you," Johann shares in his TED Talk, which has been viewed seventeen million times. "It won't be your Facebook friends who help you turn it around. It'll be your flesh and blood friends, who you have deep and nuanced and textured face-to-face relationships with."

After interviewing hundreds of twenty- and thirty-somethings about their social lives, I've learned that the path to living a happy and joyful life is making new friends and deepening relationships with old ones. The science agrees. In her in-depth study of the evolution and biology of friendship, science journalist Lydia Denworth reveals that social connections play a vital role in our health, influencing everything from our cardiovascular system to our immune system. People with close friends are happier, healthier, and live longer than people who lack strong social bonds.

In one of the longest studies ever done on adult happiness, researchers at Harvard found that *healthy relationships* are the key to a long and healthy life. The longitudinal study tracked the health of Harvard sophomores, beginning in 1938 during the Great Depression. "When we gathered everything we knew about them at age fifty, it wasn't their middle-age cholesterol levels that predicted how they were going to grow old," says Robert Waldinger, a professor of psychiatry at Harvard Medical School and director of the study, in his TED Talk. "It was how satisfied they were in their relationships. The people who were the most satisfied in their relationships at age fifty were the healthiest at age eighty." Warren Buffett, one of the wealthiest and most powerful men in the world, agrees. His number one measure for success in life is "Do the people you care about love you back?"

Whenever I get lonely, I think of my dear friend Levi Felix and I feel a little bit better. Levi started Camp Grounded, a summer camp for adults that brings together people in nature for a digital detox. At camp, we don't use digital technology, we don't talk about work, we use nicknames instead of real names, we don't talk about what time it is, we don't use drugs or alcohol, and we don't ask people how old they are. The result is a community where people can show up as their true selves and connect authentically. I was a counselor at thirteen different Camp Groundeds, serving more than three thousand people in the beautiful woods of northern California, North Carolina, New York, and Texas. I saw what happens when people are given the time and space to be vulnerable and courageous, or *vulnerageous* as we call it at camp.

In 2016, Levi was diagnosed with a stage IV glioblastoma, a brain tumor. Before his diagnosis, he was busy as ever speaking at conferences, growing Camp Grounded to reach more people across the country, and beginning to write his first book, tentatively titled *The Humanifesto: A Field Guide for Planet Earth*. He was having calls with his literary agent in New York City trying to sell his book to publishers just days before he was sent to UCSF hospital for brain surgery. We had even talked about renting a cabin in the woods for a week so he could have focused time for writing.

Levi never got to finish his book; he died of brain cancer one year after his diagnosis. He was thirty-two years old, and I miss him every single day. They say you can measure a person's life by the number of lives they touch. I think we can measure Levi's life by the number of beautiful souls he brought together. I think we can measure Levi's life by how many beautiful experiences he helped us share, not online or on an app, but with each other, in person, face-to-face, in nature, and in real life.

It was Levi, not Facebook, who taught me what a meaningful social interaction really is. Levi taught me that when I get older, I want to be able to look back and say with certainty that I spent as much time as possible being present, offscreen, outside, under the sun, playing with a new friend, swimming in a river, dancing for hours, listening to someone play the guitar, singing as loud as I can, laughing, running around like a child, holding a chair over my head, standing under a redwood tree, wearing ridiculous pajamas to breakfast, writing in my journal, making art, meditating, watching the sunset, sleeping under the stars, falling for a crush, kissing a crush, getting my heart broken by a crush, experiencing every single experience there is and everything I didn't even know existed—today, not tomorrow.

Levi taught me how to "like" things in real life, not on a digital wall.

Levi taught me that the road to connection is spending time with others offline, when no one is watching and when the story is happening in real time, not on Instagram. His legacy is that voice inside my own brain that from time to time will say, "Real quick, Smiley, get off your phone and go play with your friends."

Levi's legacy is the revolutionary act of finding human connection in the digital age, and this book is an attempt to keep my friend's torch lit and be a beacon for my own loneliness. I may have lost my friend, but I don't want to lose everything he taught me.

Toward this end, I asked the people in my life who make me feel most alive to share their own practices for sustaining friendship. I wondered: *What does it mean to actually be friends with someone in a moment when we're spending more time than ever on social media? What rituals make friendships thrive in the digital age? How can friendship become more contagious? Is it possible to reclaim friendship as an offline activity while also using technology to bring us closer together instead of further apart? What does the COVID-19 pandemic teach us about the power of building healthy relationships in the midst of social turmoil and uncertainty?*

Along the way, I interviewed loneliness experts, public health researchers, clinical psychologists, community builders, friendship experts, and many good friends of mine who know how to make me happy. What I learned was rather simple: spending more time with your friends is the best cure for the loneliness epidemic that we have. The rituals, habits, and exercises shared in this book will help you create meaningful connections, make new friends, stay in touch with old friends, deepen relationships, and become a better friend. They'll help you build a healthier relationship with technology and discover how to make virtual interactions more human. Moreover, they'll help you foster connection and belonging in an increasingly isolated, angry, and polarized digital world.

These exercises are intentionally simple; doing them is where the real work lies—my hope is that you can incorporate as many as possible into your daily practice. Think of this as a cookbook for friendship in the age of loneliness; pick it up whenever you miss your friends, whenever you need a spoonful of connection with your morning coffee (or matcha), and jump around to the recipes that are calling to you. Make this guide work for you.

I've organized this guide into six sections. Each one is based on an important lesson I learned about friendship while writing this book:

**1. Be more playful.** The road to loneliness is paved with comparison. The road to connection is paved with play. Channel your inner child. Try new things. Get curious. Ask thoughtful questions. Real friendship happens offscreen, when no one is watching. All the good shit happens in between Instagram posts. The need to capture every feeling, every moment, is robbing us of actually feeling what the moment has to offer. We are chasing these life-changing Instagrammable experiences, but

*Real friendship happens offscreen, when no one is watching.*

being awake and present for tiny, mundane, routine, day-to-day magical moments—with the people we love most—is what matters most. Play with your friends as much as you possibly can.

**2. Be a better friend.** An honest friendship is a healthy friendship. Come as you are. Talk about the hard stuff, not just the fun stuff. Find time and space to listen. Remember to ask your friends, *What's actually going on in your life? How are you really doing? Are you okay? How can I support you?* It's okay to feel lonely—even if you have lots of social connections. It's okay to be sad sometimes. It's okay not to want to hang out or be friends with someone. It's okay to say no. It's okay not to know the answers.

**3. Invest in friendship.** Friendship is an investment. Friendship is a choice. Friendship is a risk. Friendship takes time and energy and work. You can't swipe right or press a LIKE button or send an emoji to find meaningful connection. Meaningful connection does not happen overnight. Start small. Build intimacy slowly. Share your gifts. Create a reciprocal cycle of mentorship among friends. Going deep with a few close friends is more important than meeting scores of new people or having lots of Facebook friends.

**4. Stay in touch.** Being busy is not an excuse for not staying in touch. Pick up the phone and call. Invite your friends to hang out more often. Be proactive about reaching out. There's a good chance your friend who is "killing it" by the looks of things on social media is actually struggling with self-worth, depression, stress, burnout, and loneliness. There's a good chance your friend who, by the looks of things on social media is doing better than everyone else, is in fact struggling more than everyone else. Tell your friends you love them—all the time.

**5. Embrace ritual.** Rituals foster meaning, connection, and transformation. They deepen your friendships. The more creative you get about how you spend time with your people, the more nourishing those relationships are going to be. Go on overnight adventures where you can be really present together. Go on platonic friend dates where you dress up, surprise your friend, give them flowers, and buy them dinner. For men: be intentional about how you spend time with other men; seek out male friendships where you can be vulnerable, open up, and talk about your emotions. Whether it's a nightly gratitude text to a friend, a Tuesday lunch date, or an annual weekend in nature, establish traditions that make you come back to the people and places you love most.

**6. Be a minister for loneliness in your community.** In 2018, Britain appointed a Minister for Loneliness to help combat widespread loneliness as a public health concern. It would be nice if every country in the world had a Minister for Loneliness or a Department of Human Connection, but this seems unlikely. It became abundantly clear during the pandemic—especially in the United States—that no one is coming to save us. We can't wait for the government to solve loneliness or believe the false promise that tech companies are going to bring us closer together; we have to become human connection agents in our own communities. Seek to understand the perspectives of people who come from different backgrounds. Join communities that believe in the beauty of your dreams. Always ask how you can pass the torch: host gatherings, share opportunities, volunteer your time, redistribute resources, and be an inclusive and engaged citizen. Human connection is healthy for you, and healthy for the planet.

If you want to reclaim friendship, if you want to spend less time scrolling and more than 4 percent of your time in the company of people who will make you happier, you've come to the right book. Let's play together.

PART ONE

# *Be More Playful*

# MAKE A FRIEND MAP

When I began writing a book about friendship in the digital age, I reminisced about the time in my life when I felt most surrounded by real friends: college.

I was a freshman at Wesleyan University in 2001, and most of us didn't even have cell phones yet. We used landlines. Yeah, landlines! I remember having a sheet of paper on my desk with all my friends' phone extensions. And once that sheet of paper was filled, that was pretty much it on making new friends. It was like, "Well, I don't have any more room on my phone extension list, so maybe next semester we can hang out."

If you didn't make plans to meet up with your friend before going out, chances are you'd spend the rest of the night looking for them. There was no iMessage. We just had whiteboards outside our dorm rooms where someone could leave a message for you: "DUDE, WHERE ARE YOU?!" Then, you'd go to your friend's dorm room and write on their board: "DUDE, WHERE ARE *YOUUUUUUU*? I'm here!!!"

This back-and-forth could last a few hours—or even a whole week-end. It was like the original Snapchat snap streak.

Of course, you'd eventually find your friends roaming the streets looking for a house party. You'd be wandering campus with a pack of ten people and run into another pack of ten people. Someone would scream: "I heard there's a party at 42 Home Ave!" "I heard 60 Fountain Ave!" "84 High Street!" "Party on Vine Street!" Sometimes you'd get there, and there wasn't even a party happening! People would be like, "Nah man, there's no party here, get the hell off my porch! I have a midterm tomorrow!"

There was something very meaningful about that pre–cell phone and pre–social media time. I felt very present. I knew who my friends were. I spent a lot of time with my close friends, listening to scratched Weezer CDs and Napster playlists, trying to study in the library, smoking joints on the Hill, loving life.

Fast-forward twenty years, and my friends from college are spread out all around the country. Most of them are married and have children. Meanwhile, I spent much of the past year feeling lonely. I meet new people all the time, but sometimes I'm not sure who my real friends are. I wanted to reach out to some of my old friends from college, but I didn't know where to start.

I decided to follow the advice from a buddy to make a friend map. "It's like that LCD Soundsystem song, 'All My Friends,'" he explained. "Where the hell are all my friends tonight?!" So, I took out a piece of paper and, as best I could, drew a rough map of the United States. Then, I started jotting down names of all my close friends, placing them loosely where they lived. I listed my close friends who live in other countries as well.

Based on my friend's advice, I put my Friend Map on my wall above my desk. Every now and then, I pick one friend I haven't spoken to in a long time, and I send them a postcard about a fun memory I have of us spending time together back in the day. I call these my Back in the Day Postcards. Just looking at that map above my desk reminds me of all the people out there who care about me, and the simple gesture of reaching out adds a smile to my week.

# TRADE SCREEN TIME FOR FRIEND TIME

Camp Grounded's motto was "Disconnect to reconnect." While some critics incorrectly assumed this meant camp was about escaping technology, Levi was not a Luddite—he checked his iPhone just as much as you or I do. He viewed the experience of taking a four-day digital detox as a step toward building a more mindful relationship with our devices. It wasn't about escape or retreat or going to camp as much as it was about reconnection and balance when you *came home* from camp.

Levi often criticized apps that used a never-ending onslaught of push notifications to keep us glued to our phones, rather than using technology to help us spend more time offline with the people we love most. He would often caution us, noting that 60 percent of people admit being addicted to their devices, the average person checks their phone 150 times a day, 30 percent of people admit to hiding from friends and family to check social media, one in ten people check their phone during sex, and one in six phones have traces of *E. coli* fecal matter on their screen because people can't be away from their phones long enough to go to the bathroom.

Before you handed over your iPhone for a weekend of fun in the woods at Camp Grounded, you first entered a cultish tech-check tent run by the (made-up) International Institute of Digital Detoxification (IIODD), recited a six-line pledge that you wouldn't be tricked by phantom cell phone vibrations in your pocket, then watched a five-minute video with talking sock puppets who asked, "Is shexting really worth it?" before finally turning over your phone to members of the IIODD wearing hazmat suits.

All too often it's our devices telling us what to do. We click on a push notification, "Maria commented on your Facebook post," and three hours later, we've gone back and forth with Maria and six other people we don't even know on the comment thread, and even worse, we have thirteen new tabs open, with articles and videos we're saving to check out later. Our Saturday afternoon has disappeared, our body is tense, and our eyes are exhausted. Tristan Harris, technology ethicist and cofounder of the Center for Humane Technology, has called our devices attention-grabbing slot machines hijacking our minds. "There's a hidden goal driving the direction of all of the technology we make, and that goal is the race for our attention," Tristan warns.

During the early days of the pandemic, calls to shelter in place slowed my life dramatically. I was no longer traveling all the time, flying from city to city, going from event to event, or meeting new people. I noticed that I no longer had energy for everyone in my life, and I had to focus my very limited pool of energy available on the people and tasks I cared most about. Checking the news became arduous and overwhelming. I spent far less time posting on social media, self-promoting, buying things, and being "busy," and I spent far more time taking masked walks in the neighborhood, cooking dinner with my partner, talking to my family, and enjoying moments like watching my nephew take his first steps. I chose prioritizing my *friends* over worrying about my *followers*. Needless to say, I felt a lot more grounded.

Why did it take a pandemic for me to slow down? How can we create more opportunities to focus our attention on things we actually care about? Sure, you can go on a ten-day silent meditation retreat or a weekend-long digital detox in the woods, but that's not often possible.

So, here's a simple and fun practice for adding more presence to your days: trade screen time for friend time.

In your phone settings, click on SCREEN TIME and check the average daily amount of time you spent on your phone and your total screen time for the week. Note your daily average of phone "pickups." Click on the "social networking" category, and note the number of hours you spent in the past week on apps like TikTok, Instagram, Twitter, Facebook, Snapchat, etc. Write down these numbers on a Post-it, and put the Post-it on your bathroom mirror so it's the first thing you see every morning when you wake up. Next week, I challenge you to spend the same amount of time you spent on social networking apps on your phone hanging out with or calling one or two friends from your Friend Map. Don't think of it as homework—I'm just asking you to kick it with your friends! For bonus points, disable all your push notifications for the week, and notice how much more attention you have for people on your Friend Map.

# QUESTION WHAT IT MEANS TO BE A GROWN-UP

When I think about the power of play, I think about one of my best friends, Brady Gill, aka Honey Bear. Brady was the head counselor and assistant director at Camp Grounded and has been going to summer camp for more than thirty years (he's only missed three summers since he was six!). Brady's been on staff and directed summer camps for kids like Camp Tawonga and Camp Galileo, and these days he runs Custom Camps, bringing play and team-building activities to adults at companies and corporate retreats.

Brady told me that the power of play is transformative and liberating; it breaks down our misconceptions of what it means to be an adult in a success-driven, status-obsessed society. "Especially in America, we both create and have created for us rules of what it means to be a grown-up," Brady explains. "Our rules around being a grown-up are really centered around success, progress, and achievement; as in, adults are supposed to have all the answers. But it's an unrealistic expectation, and because of it, we don't give ourselves much permission to learn or grow because that's admitting that we're not successful or achieving."

Brady contrasted this unrealistic expectation with our rules for children. With kids, the rules are just the opposite. With kids, failure is celebrated. With kids, everything is an opportunity to teach, learn, and grow; that's the point of your existence, that's why you're in school. But at some point, that childlike wonder is replaced with an expectation that we're supposed to know it all, which is really unfortunate because the point of adulthood should also be to keep learning and growing all the time. As Brady says, "We enter adulthood half-baked, and no one keeps the oven on for us."

Having summer camp for grown-ups helps keep the oven on. At Camp Grounded, we used to assign every (adult) camper a village with fifteen other campers and a counselor. The job of the counselor, like the job of a counselor at kids' summer camp, is to keep the campers safe. Not just physically safe but emotionally safe. Their job is to be their campers' friend and help them make new friends. Their job is to validate their campers, to celebrate all the ways they are awesome, to tell them where they can grow, and to hold them accountable in that process. The role of the camp counselor is similar to that of a great teacher, coach, mentor, or sibling: to have someone's back and validate them for who they really are. Kids need that type of encouragement, and the simple truth is, adults do, too.

Brady told me that when he was a young kid, he was really insecure. I find it hard to believe that someone like Brady could have ever been insecure. When we're together, Brady is usually leading a game of Rock Paper Scissors Rockstar, where hundreds of people are screaming at the top of their lungs; but Brady was an insecure kid who thought everyone else had it together and that something was wrong with him. Being at summer camp helped him realize that he wasn't alone, that *everyone* feels like they're faking it, that *no one* knows what they are doing, that *everyone* is freaked out and just doing their best. This realization was a breakthrough for Brady, and he's been bringing the magic of summer camp to adults ever since. Here are a few things he's learned along the way:

**1. Adults need permission to play.** One of the reasons it's so easy for kids to play is that we set very clear expectations for kids. We say:

"It's playtime now!" or "You can do whatever you want during recess," or "This is a space to make mistakes and learn." This way, kids know *exactly* what to do. We give them permission to mess up and not know the answers. We don't do that for adults.

**2. Adults need to know they aren't alone in feeling scared.** On the first day of Camp Grounded a few years ago, Brady shared with the entire camp that at least 50 percent of campers (more than one hundred people) reported on their intake forms that they felt like they wouldn't make friends or that this experience wouldn't be right for them. By naming the discomfort right off the bat, Brady made campers feel less alone, made it okay for people to feel left out and awkward, and created a shared bond around feeling scared together, feeling insecure together, and feeling like we were all going to get through the experience together.

**3. Adults need help making friends.** There are so few times in our adult lives where there's a clear invitation to make new friends. There are speed-dating events and online dating for romantic relationships, but there's very little of that for friendship. On the first afternoon of Camp Grounded, campers are given two hours of "bonding time" in their village, where the explicit goal is to help people meet each other and become friends. There's a buddy bench where you can go sit, and it's an invitation that you would like to talk to someone. There's a norm to always sit in an open circle rather than a closed circle, so there's an invitation for someone to join. When someone new arrives at the Talent Show, people scream out, "One new friend! One new friend!" just so the person doesn't have to sit alone.

Brady told me that the morning after the first day at Camp Tawonga, all of the supervisors sit down for a meeting and go through a list of every single kid at camp and ask, "Have they made a friend yet?" If the answer is no, the staff's goal becomes to make sure they've made a friend by the end of the day.

**4. Adults need to play more games.** Brady told me that any game or icebreaker is a tiny moment where there's a new set of rules that are superbly different from our normal social interactions. These "breaks in the rules" allow adults to question the world around them. For example, when people arrive at Camp Grounded and are told they can't use their digital devices, can't talk about work, and can't use their real name, it immediately transports them to a place that feels different, and often more liberating, than their normal day-to-day existence.

A game, however brief, is a mini-moment of breaking out of the matrix. When you're playing an icebreaker with Brady called "Quack!" your goal is to meet as many people as possible in the span of thirty seconds, as you double high-five them and then bend over in between your legs to scream out, "Quack!" while trying to remember everyone's name. A game like this may seem silly—and certainly is—but when someone leaves camp and returns to the real world, they might question why the hell they spend every Monday morning walking down the street with their head buried in an iPhone or why the hell they don't know a single thing about most of their coworkers. "We all have these 'rule ceilings,' and if you've been in a place or had an experience like camp, where every rule you thought was important turns out to be imaginary, it begins to create cracks in your ceiling," says Brady.

# TRY NEW THINGS

Imagine if we spent less time worrying and more time trying new things. This is Molly Sonsteng's life mission. Molly is a "producer of play" and the founder of Caveday, where people gather for facilitated deep work sessions, and First Time Out, a variety show for first-time performers. By creating a loving and supportive environment, First Time Out allows grown-ups to try new things in a low-stakes environment. Since starting the event in New York City, Molly has hosted twenty-five shows with more than three hundred first-timers onstage.

Molly told me about a woman named Claire who had written countless songs and had nowhere to share them until she came to First Time Out. The energy in the room helped her forget about her nerves, and a year later Claire had recorded a full-length album and now performs several times a month.

"As children, we engage in play so openly and authentically," Molly explains. "As we age, though, we build up a shield and resistance to play. We build layers that are either too cool or too professional or too successful. But there's a moment when we allow ourselves to really play and return to our inner child. At that moment, the layers fall away. We spend a lot of time as young people talking about what we want to be when we grow up, but as grown-ups it's amazing how often all we really want is to be kids again.

"My husband is an amateur magician, and he believes 'real magic is the suspension of one's disbelief.' It's not a coin actually disappearing; it's when that shielded, professional adult believes for just one split moment that the coin may truly have disappeared. While this anecdote refers to magic, it's the same moment I seek when turning someone on to play. It's as quick as a snap of the finger. It's as brief as turning on a light switch. I can see it in their eyes. And that's when I know they're willing to play along."

Molly's words remind me that there is power in being the magician who turns on the switch. There is power in trying something for the first time. There is power in getting weird first. When you see someone get onstage at First Time Out and do something they've never done before, everyone else in the room feels liberated to break out of their shell. When you play along, you inspire others to play along, too—and when everyone plays along, everyone is weird; and when everyone is weird, everyone is themselves; and when everyone is themselves, everyone belongs.

In her book *The Art of Gathering*, Priya Parker teaches us that transformative gatherings create a temporary alternative world. "The amazing thing about gatherings is that, for a limited, temporary moment in time, you get to create a moment where you get to set the rules," Priya shares in an interview. These rules—however simple, like telling someone what they should bring or if they should wear a costume—inform how your guests show up. By having a simple rule (this night is for first-time performers), First Time Out immediately creates a temporary world full of moments of courage and bravery for folks like Claire to overcome their fears and make their own magic.

Molly shared three simple ways all of us can be more playful in our daily lives:

**1. Do something new every day.** Put cinnamon on your ice cream. Wear your watch on the opposite arm. Do five jumping jacks in front of the mirror. Doing something different each day is a wonderful way to help distinguish one day from the next. Plus, as Molly reminds me, it's fun finding new things to do each day!

**2. Ask different questions.** When meeting someone new, ask different questions. Molly starts out simple with something like "How was your day?" You'd be surprised how rare that question really is when meeting someone new for the very first time. Another idea: "What was the silliest thing that happened to you today?" Work up to the old classics like "What do you do?" or "Where are you from?" Even if you're genuinely interested in what someone does for work, beginning a conversation differently kicks off a lighter and more playful tone. Which (you guessed it) makes for a more connected and meaningful conversation.

**3. Carry a trinket.** Find something small you love and carry it with you. Molly carries a spinning top. Always. Everywhere she goes. Not only does this serve as a reminder to be lighthearted, it's a great toy to pull out when she's waiting for a meeting to begin, rather than staring at her phone (not to mention it being a terrific conversation piece). Your trinket should be small enough to fit in your wallet or backpack.

# Twenty Questions More Interesting Than "What Do You Do?"

● · ● ·

What's something unexpected that happened to you this week?

What's the most memorable concert you've ever been to?

When you can't fall asleep, what is keeping you up?

Who in your life makes you laugh out loud?

What's the worst date you've ever been on?

What was a beautiful moment you recently had that wasn't captured on social media?

What's the last album you listened to the whole way through?

If you could travel anywhere tomorrow, where would you go?

What's your favorite thing to do when you're alone?

What does your dream home or apartment look like?

What was the best platonic sleepover you've ever had?

What's a creative project you want to bring into the world?

What would your campaign slogan be if you ran for president?

If you could be a character in a TV show for a day,
who would you be and why?

What does "doing nothing" mean to you?

How is your heart right now?

Do you have a spiritual practice?

Who is a good friend from high school you're no longer
in touch with and why?

When's the last time you cried?

What did you learn during the COVID-19 pandemic that
you will never forget?

———

Need more conversation starters? Check out "The 36 Questions
That Lead to Love," referenced in Mandy Len Catron's popular "Modern Love" essay, which refers to a psychological study
by Arthur Aron and others about whether intimacy between two
people can be accelerated by having them answer a series of
questions that get more intimate over time. My favorite question
is #33: "If you were to die this evening with no opportunity to
communicate with anyone, what would you most regret not having told someone? Why haven't you told them yet?"

# BECOME A SHERIFF
# OF GOOD TIMES

At Camp Grounded, we had a Sheriff of Good Times who was in charge of making sure everyone was having a good time. Our sheriff's nickname was Bubbles, and Bubbles would go around camp and approach anyone who looked like they were struggling a little. Sometimes he'd check in to see if they were okay. Sometimes he'd just sit and listen while they talked. And sometimes he'd invite them to check out something fun that was happening. The most important thing Bubbles did was make people feel welcome and celebrated for who they were.

Affirmation is largely undervalued in our society. We're so used to hearing what we're not good at. The simple act of telling someone that they can be themselves, that they're already doing a great job, that they are okay exactly the way they are is incredibly powerful.

What are ways that you can become a Sheriff of Good Times in your daily routine? Maybe you carry gold star stickers and hand them out when you see people doing something awesome. Or stand outside a grocery store and see if someone needs help taking their grocery bags to their car. Or next time you're in line at a coffee shop, buy the person behind you their coffee and tell them they have to pay it forward tomorrow. Or next time you go to the airport, carry a deck of cards with you and see if someone wants to play rummy while you wait for your flight. Or give out frozen ice pops in the summer. Or just offer to listen to someone tell you about their day.

I often think about what it would be like if our police spent less time policing people and more time welcoming people who feel left out or need an extra hand. We don't need more sheriffs, we need more Sheriffs of Good Times.

# FIND SOMETHING THAT MAKES YOU FEEL WHOLE

A few years ago, I called up my friend and mentor, Dev Aujla. Dev runs Catalog, an agency that provides strategic advisory and recruiting services to companies that make money and do good. He is also the founder of DreamNow, a charitable organization that has helped more than fifty thousand young people organize and start community projects. When I called Dev, I was struggling with a professional conundrum: a feeling of stress and anxiety over having to monetize my work. I had just published my first book, and I was at a crossroads in my career. I told Dev I didn't want to spend all my time managing my email newsletter or being an internet marketer or finding a way to optimize "selling myself"; I wanted to spend more time with people I cared about. Dev gave me simple advice: "Don't do what you think you are supposed to do. Don't do what makes you feel broken inside. Find something that makes you feel whole. Find something that makes you feel *so f\*cking good* inside."

This advice was a breakthrough for me. Instead of spending my energy online, staring at a computer screen, worried about click-through rates and "building my following," I decided to do something that actually made me feel good. I doubled down on my public speaking business and started traveling all across the country and around the world to speak. Five years since our conversation, public speaking is my full-time job; it brings me joy, and I make far more money than I probably ever would trying to monetize my Instagram posts.

A few months after that conversation, I called Dev to thank him for his timely and spot-on advice. This time, though, Dev needed my help. He was looking for a new literary agent who really believed in him and his second book, *50 Ways to Get a Job*, all about the power of non-linear career thinking. I mentioned to him that I really liked my agent and would be happy to connect them. Dev and my agent hit it off, and Dev ended up getting a book deal for his project. That's how you know a mentor–protégé relationship (or any friendship) is truly meaningful; both people have something to give (and receive) from the other.

The next time I spoke to Dev, he had taken his own advice to heart. He had followed his love for people pursuing nonlinear journeys and opened his own little library in a windowless room on the ground floor of a coworking space in Brooklyn, New York. Sorted Library celebrates nonlinear thinking by creating small reading rooms that are full re-creations of famous creative people's libraries. Visitors to Sorted Library then create their own miniature collection of three to five books from within these libraries around varied themes of inquiry, like "How to Love the World," "Books My Mom Teaches to High Schoolers," "Impacts of Our Design Decisions," "The Voices We Hear in Solitude," "Me-search," and "Eating at the End of the World."

I congratulated Dev on following his dream and building Sorted Library from scratch. He told me the even better news that he had fallen in love. He had met Liz once for a work coffee and then invited her and her coworkers to the library one day. Liz's team couldn't make it, but Liz showed up. As Dev recalls, "I was in my zone working in the library. In that setting, there was so much space to lose yourself in the books and have a conversation. We talked for three hours that day."

After Liz left the library, Dev texted his brother, "I think I met somebody." He didn't know this at the time, but Liz also texted a friend that she had met someone special.

On their tenth date, Dev and Liz went on a ten-day trip across the North Atlantic on a cargo ship from Halifax to Liverpool. "Every day on the ship felt like a month of dating in New York," Dev wrote. "Over those ten days, we spent more than 160 hours awake together, shared two dozen meals, and made out more than the average couple does in five months. By the third day, I told Liz I loved her. By the fifth, we were talking about the future. By the eighth, we were arguing."

A few months later, Dev and Liz were engaged. I asked Dev if he thought the library had anything to do with their romance. "Definitely. The project just felt so good. There was an ease to the way it happened; I got the space for free; a bookstore gave me thousands of books. I felt like I was going to meet someone, even if most days I was spending five hours a day by myself in a windowless room. I lost track of time. I was in flow. I felt like myself, and when you feel like yourself, you can actually meet that person."

By following his own unique curiosity and listening to his internal compass, opening a library that was likely never going to bring him fame or fortune, Dev found wholeness, a sense of self, someone who could see him for who he really was, and that thing all of us are looking for: love.

# HUG MORE, HUG LONGER

Creating more comfort around physical touch makes all the difference. The oxytocin release that comes from hugging—especially one of those hugs that lasts a little longer than you're used to—can decrease heart rate; cause a drop in stress hormones; and help heal loneliness, isolation, and anger. According to research at the University of North Carolina, women who are frequently hugged have lower blood pressure than those who are not, and a study by Carnegie Mellon University found that people who received regular hugs had fewer flu symptoms than those who were hugged less frequently. As philosophy professor Stephen Asma writes, "Real bonding is more biological than psychological and requires physical contact. The emotional entanglement of real friendship produces oxytocin and endorphins in the brains and bodies of friends—cementing them together in ways that are more profound than other relationships."

Platonic touch among men—particularly in a culture like America, where physical touch among men is often stigmatized—is good for men and good for society. A study in the journal *Adolescence* that looked at forty-nine cultures found that "the cultures that exhibited minimal physical affection toward their young children had significantly higher rates of adult violence."

One of my best friends, Gabe Prager, gives the best bear hugs I've ever had in my life. He doesn't just give one of those awkward man hugs—you know, the kind where two men are afraid of demonstrating how much they actually love each other—the kind where two men seem to be saying, "Yo, what up, good to see you, man, how you been, man?—I drink beer, you drink beer, too? I like sports, you like sports, too, right? I'm not gonna get too close because people might think we're lovers, and I'm still afraid of being called 'gay' 'cause I was called 'gay' in fifth grade because our society is homophobic and every image of love I've ever seen in magazines and TV shows is of a man and a woman hugging."

Instead, Gabe squeezes you like he means it. He squeezes you like he loves you. He squeezes you like he isn't afraid of what people will say when they see two men hugging for a minute on the street, because it should be completely normal and accepted and encouraged to see two men hugging (or kissing!) on the street. I love when my male friends squeeze me like they love me, because I love them, too. Gabe's thirty-second hug says, "I missed you, brother. You're the only person in the world who matters right now. I'm so happy you're in my life. I need you in my life. You need me in your life. I'm here for you. We're here for each other."

My partner's great aunt Deb, who is ninety-seven years old, told me that what she missed most after her husband of sixty-four years died was physical touch. This yearning became even harder during COVID-19. Deb told me that what she was really missing were hugs and being touched. She took solace in the fact that whenever her family would visit to help her plant window boxes or prepare food, even though they couldn't physically get closer than six feet, they would spend a few moments hugging themselves. The self-hug wasn't the same, but it provided enough oxytocin to get by.

My buddy Jonah shared that he was grateful he was living far away from his close friends during quarantine, because it would have been impossible not to hug them. "Hugs are my friendship ritual," he said. "I have a unique hug for each of my buddies when I see them."

Next time you see someone you care about, ask them if they want a thirty-second hug, and hug them like you mean it.

*Hug your friends
like you mean it.*

# GET INTO YOUR BODY

Kyla Sokoll-Ward, a loneliness expert and host of the podcast *Conversations That Don't Suck*, believes that the future of friendship lies in becoming more attuned to the ways we want to be in connection to others. In other words, it's not enough to have relationships; it's about knowing what you *need* from those relationships. Sometimes we need a friend to meet us where we are to truly understand us. "It's okay to be picky about the quality of how we're connecting with our friends, so we can feel truly seen and known by the people closest to us. It's okay to expect more of others," Kyla says.

My friend Bailey Robinson's journey to more meaningful friendships was a six-year journey of self-exploration and emotional healing. "When it came time to be held in my pain, my relationships weren't reciprocal," she describes. "I was playing the role of Mama Bear for other people, but others weren't emotionally there for me."

It took Bailey a long time to figure out how to ask for what she needed. She started by attending connection events, showing up and saying whatever was present, realizing that she wasn't alone and that so many other people were starving for a deeper, more spiritual connection. "I just started with my voice," Bailey recalls. "I went to so many connection events. I couldn't do this alone. I just needed to show up." Bailey started running an event called Feelings Playtime, where people would share their feelings and needs.

In showing up, Bailey learned more about herself and the types of people she wanted to be around and the types of friends she had to take a much-needed break from. "In order to learn about yourself, you need to be mirrored by as many people as possible," Bailey says. "Therapists, friends, communities. You want more people around because it will reflect more parts of you."

Bailey also learned how much of her transformation was somatic: not just in her mind but in her body. "My self-exploration journey started six years ago," Bailey recalls. "I had read fifty business self-help books. I was comfortable in my mind, in the business world, but the real transformational process was an embodiment practice for me. Being in the body with my feelings. . . . The more embodied I got, the easier self-connection was. The easier choosing the right connections became."

As Bailey started to become more aware of the feelings in her body, she got closer to the type of friendship connection she was looking for. She started attending intentional gatherings like Camp Grounded, Soul Play (a four-day festival focused on heart-opening connection, personal expansion, invigorating yoga, and blissful dance), and going to ecstatic dance on Sunday mornings. When she first went to ecstatic dance, she felt so uncomfortable watching all the other people dancing low to the floor, looking like they were possessed. "I was like, what the hell are all those crazy people on the floor doing?!" she says. "And then I was one of them. It became my home."

Bailey gave me three lessons she had learned on her journey to more embodied connection that seem relevant for modern friendship:

1. Put yourself in the places and spaces with people who are further along in the **self-discovery** journey than you are, and the transformation will happen.

2. Do anything you can do to feel a **sense of safety**. Every breakthrough Bailey's had is because she felt an extreme sense of safety—in the place, in the person, and eventually within herself.

3. Build **self-compassion** into your practice. Try to meet yourself where you are and others where they are. Be thankful, not a know-it-all.

# WHEREVER YOU GO, BRING AN OFFERING

Have you ever sat around your house, scrolling Instagram, seeing all the cool things your friends are doing and hoping, wishing, praying that someone would text you and want to hang out with you? I certainly have, and it sucks.

I listened to a podcast interview with Radha Agrawal, author of *Belong*, who offered a far better practice than sitting around waiting for your friends to do something for you. Radha, who cofounded Daybreaker, which has put on hundreds of sober morning dance parties in twenty-five cities around the globe for a community of half a million people, shared that one of her best pieces of advice for building your community is to always show up and be of service. Whatever it is—cooking a meal, listening, or even taking out the trash—when you add value, people pay attention.

Chances are, if you're not excited about showing up from a place of service in your community, that community isn't the right fit for you. When I first started working at Camp Grounded, I knew I had found my people because I would spend hours setting up chairs and carrying heavy tables across camp. I remember it was 1 a.m., we had been moving things around all day, and I wasn't even that tired. In other words, the work didn't feel like *work* because I was so excited to contribute to camp. If you're actually excited to do manual labor, if you're truly and genuinely excited to be of service, that's a sign that you're in the right place.

I also experienced this at Burning Man, where a decommodified city in the middle of the Black Rock Desert in Nevada is built from scratch every year in late August. Burning Man runs on the spirit of gifting. The only things you can buy with money in Black Rock City are coffee and ice; everything else is shared in a gift economy. As the Burning Man website states, "In order to preserve the spirit of gifting, our community seeks to create social environments that are unmediated by commercial sponsorships, transactions, or advertising. We stand ready to protect our culture from such exploitation. We resist the substitution of consumption for participatory experience."

When I was at Burning Man, in the span of a few days, I was given all of the following by complete strangers: watermelon, a cold pickle, a piece of French toast with powdered sugar and cinnamon, a bacon Bloody Mary, truffle salt popcorn, a red velvet cupcake, a cone of orange sherbet, *jugo de naranja*, iced chai, lavender mist, and a steam bath.

Levi always used to say that the "sharing economy" was sharing a handwritten note, not charging someone $345 to stay at your apartment or $27 to take a ride in your car. All too often, our profit-driven world is transaction-based: you give someone money, and they give you something in return. When you give without asking for something in return, you break down barriers and you change lives. You make people happy. You inspire people to pay it forward. You remind people what it means to feel alive.

Contrary to what a "gift shop" might have you believe, you don't need a reason to give somebody a present. It doesn't need to be someone's birthday or Father's Day or a wedding to give someone something. You don't even need to know someone to give them a present. It's amazing what can happen when we open ourselves to giving and receiving. We stop judging. We start to see others as equals and understand there's a collective consciousness at the root of humanity.

A great way to foster connection with strangers is to bring a gift or offering when you go out. Maybe it's a chocolate chip cookie, or maybe it's a musical instrument, a poem, a flower, candles, lavender or sage or some herbs from your garden, or a handwritten note. Your offering can be something small and silly; the important thing is that you're adding a gift to the mix.

# OPEN YOUR WORLD

Have you ever been scared to move to a new city because you're scared of starting over, because you're scared of making new friends as an adult? I certainly have. Since graduating college, I've lived in Boston; Brooklyn; Buenos Aires; Washington, DC; San Francisco; and now Oakland. I've often felt like I don't have the bandwidth to start over again; I can't imagine another move, so I'm going to make the best of what I have right now.

This type of mentality can be an obstacle, especially if you really are ready to make a change, start a new job, or move on from your current living situation. "Whenever I hear people say that they don't want to move to a new city because they would have to start over, I have a little sadness," my friend Joanna Miller told me. Joanna has spent a lot of time thinking about how to maintain relationships that you've already established and how to get over the fear of being the new person and meeting strangers.

Joanna lives by the axiom "A stranger is a friend you haven't met yet" and likens being around strangers to a game of chicken, where everyone is craving connection, but no one wants to be the first person to make a move. Her advice: open your world to other people.

First, **know what you enjoy doing.** You don't need to recite a list of your most impressive career achievements or be good at something you think people are going to be attracted to. Instead, double down on the things you authentically like and are into.

Second, **focus on staying present with the person you're with.** Similar to a first date, you're not asking yourself, "Do I want to spend the rest of my life with this person?" You're asking, "Am I interested in what this person has to say? Am I engaged right now? Am I having a good time?" If the answer is yes, then keep hanging with them.

Third, **open your world to other people.** Make sure you're offering things about yourself that you want others to know and that you're trying to discover things about strangers that you actually care about. First conversations with strangers can be nerve-racking. As a hack for this, Joanna has go-to questions that she always asks strangers. One is "What's something that you enjoyed doing when you were growing up but wouldn't be able to do today?" Joanna's answer: Going to record stores with her dad. If you just moved to a new city, try asking, "What's your favorite neighborhood, and what should I check out while I'm there?"

Finally, **make connecting with strangers a game.** Have a sense of adventure about it. When Joanna was studying abroad in Italy, she told herself that during the first six weeks of the program, if anyone asked her to do anything (that wasn't life-threatening), she would answer, "Yes." This led to meeting new people at a café, going to a nightclub, and learning more about her new home. Another game that Joanna used to play was called "flirting with the world," or "catching smiles." On her three-mile walk home from work, she would try to get as many strangers as possible to smile back at her. When she first started playing the game, she came on a little too strong. Her glare was a little intense, and people were scared away. But as she eased into the walk and eased into the music she was listening to on her headphones, more and more people were smiling back at her. By the end of the walk, she had caught thirty smiles from strangers.

These games helped Joanna lower her fear around engaging with strangers and become more comfortable going into new experiences. She decided to bring a sense of adventure into more aspects of her social life. Back in 2014, Joanna was feeling fed up with going to birthday dinners where people would show up at a fancy restaurant, have to overpay for dinner, and not even get to talk to the person whose birthday it was. She wanted to do something different for her birthday. One of her favorite things in the world was to watch the sun rise, so she wondered, "What if we went somewhere high up in San Francisco and watched the sun rise and had a dance party?"

Thus, the Sunrise Club was born. On the first Monday of the month, Joanna and some friends would meet on the top of Twin Peaks in San Francisco, overlooking the whole city; they would share food, wear costumes, set intentions for the month, dance, and leave in time for people to get to work. Anyone was welcome to bring their friends or new people they had just met. Joanna told me that attendees started dating, made new friends, and even held space for community members who had recently lost their friends in an accident.

Sunrise Club has continued. Joanna even went up to Twin Peaks by herself during COVID-19 for a socially distanced edition and ended up running into a stranger who was also celebrating the sunrise on Twin Peaks that morning. They ended up giving each other astrological readings.

"So many people are throwing breadcrumbs at us to connect," says Joanna. "But we are programmed to reject them. You need to reprogram yourself to see the invitations that people are offering you."

PART TWO

# *Be a Better*
# *Friend*

# BELONG TO YOURSELF FIRST

After the dance party at my friends Amber and Farhad's beautiful destination wedding in Marrakech, several friends and I stayed up very late, almost until sunrise. We were lying in a garden, staring up at the Moroccan sky high above the Atlas Mountains. You could see every star in the Milky Way.

A friend asked a question I hadn't thought about in a very long time: *"Why do you love yourself?"* We took turns answering. I said that I love my energy. I love my power to bring positivity and realness to almost any situation, any place I go, any room I'm in. I said that I love my ability to make others smile. When we're in a group, we often think about fitting in. We focus on what we think the crowd wants us to do. But the prompt made me realize that the first step is being comfortable in your own skin.

In Brené Brown's book *Braving the Wilderness*, Brené says that belonging really means belonging to yourself first. Belonging is speaking your truth. "Don't walk through the world looking for evidence that you don't belong, because you will always find it," she advises. "Don't walk through the world looking for evidence that you are not enough, because you will always find it. Our worth and our belonging are not negotiated with other people. We carry those inside of our hearts."

*Belonging* is a buzzword these days—something I hear about at every corporate conference I attend—but I first learned about belonging when I was a little kid, way back in the 1980s, from a guy named Fred. Fred Rogers, that is. I used to watch the television show *Mister Rogers' Neighborhood* every single day when I was young. My parents would record the episodes on their VHS machine, and I'd watch those tapes over and over again. I think I watched the episode where Mister Rogers visits a mushroom farm no less than ninety-seven times.

I remember once we were on a family vacation in Ohio, and I was about five years old, and we bumped into the mushroom farmer that Mr. Rogers had interviewed on the show. He was having breakfast in the lobby of the hotel where we were staying at. I ran up to him and exclaimed, "Mr. Mushroom! Mr. Mushroom! How did you get out of the TV?!"

He looked at me, smiled, and said, "Kid, you have no idea how often I get asked that question."

One of the reasons I loved *Mister Rogers' Neighborhood* so much was because it taught me at an early age that I belonged, that I was supposed to be here, that I mattered, and that my feelings mattered. When Fred Rogers was trying to secure more funding for public broadcasting and his show, he presented his work before the Senate Subcommittee on Communications in 1969, explaining: "I give an expression of care to each child. To help him realize that he is unique. I end the program by saying, 'You've made this day a special day. Just by your being you. There's no person in the world just like you, and I like you just the way you are.' And I feel if we in public television can only make it clear that feelings are mentionable and manageable, we will have done a great service for mental health."

Both Fred Rogers and Brené Brown teach us that belonging is in fact the opposite of fitting in, the opposite of saying the "right thing." It's saying what's true for you. It's knowing who you are. Before we think about showing up for our friends, it's vital we know ourselves and belong to ourselves first.

Shortly before he died in 2003, Fred Rogers quoted Henry James saying, "There are three ways to ultimate success. The first way is to be kind. The second way is to be kind. The third way is to be kind." So, what does it mean to be kind to your unique self? To like yourself just the way you are? What about yourself do you know to be true? What does it mean to love yourself?

# DESTIGMATIZE
# MENTAL HEALTH

My friend Dr. Emily Anhalt is the cofounder and chief clinical officer of Coa: A Mental Fitness Community. Dr. Anhalt, a therapist who studied psychology at the University of Michigan and attained master's and doctorate degrees in clinical psychology from the Wright Institute in Berkeley, California, is on a mission to destigmatize mental health and evangelize the value of *emotional fitness* for self-growth, friendship, and relationships, as well as for leaders and managers in the workplace.

"Here's what I mean by emotional fitness," she says. "Beyond having good coping mechanisms to deal with anxiety, depression, self-doubt, and a series of curveballs that are completely out of your control, [you] must be able to form and maintain good relationships. You must be able to communicate effectively. . . . Maintaining emotional fitness is an ongoing, proactive practice that increases self-awareness, positively affects relationships, improves leadership skills, and prevents mental and emotional struggles down the line. Think about it less like going to the doctor and more like going to the gym."

After conducting an interpretative analysis of hundreds of interviews with psychologists and entrepreneurs, Dr. Anhalt distilled her findings into seven traits of emotional fitness for leaders: self-awareness, empathy, willingness to play, curiosity, mindfulness, resilience, and effective communication.

One of the best tools available for the first trait, self-awareness, is therapy. "Starting a meditation habit, focusing on your yoga practice or journaling every day can be impactful and I love these practices. And sometimes you also need to dig deeper to get the support you need," Dr. Anhalt explains.

For decades, therapy has been thought of as something you did when you were really depressed or when you were experiencing major loss or trauma. It was seen as a service only available for the ultra-unwell or the ultra-wealthy. I can share personally that for many years I resisted seeing a therapist because I wasn't working through a major life crisis. I assumed my problems were far less important or serious than what other people were facing. But as the pandemic spread, gave me immense stress, and threatened my livelihood with the cancellation of all my speaking events, I started seeing a therapist; and it really helped me talk through my anxieties, work on myself, and communicate better with my partner. I learned I wasn't alone in feeling overburdened due to COVID-19—a third of Americans (more than one hundred million people) showed signs of clinical anxiety or depression in May 2020, according to the Census Bureau.

Therapy has taught me the value of present and active listening, an important tool for being a good friend. During my first session with my therapist, I thought to myself, "All this guy does is just sit there and listen to me. What the hell am I paying for?!" By our fourth session, I finally got it. I was like, "Ohhhhhhhhh, all this guy does is just sit there and listen to me. That's inimitable."

Having someone whose sole purpose is to hold space for your feelings is really important. "We need to shift the narrative of therapy from something you access only when you're unwell to something you proactively do to promote wellness," Dr. Anhalt says.

In conversations and interviews for this book, many people told me how valuable therapy had been for their capacity to reconnect with themselves and build healthy friendships. There are a number of online tools making it easier than ever to find a therapist, like Ayana Therapy, an app for marginalized and intersectional communities that matches users with licensed professionals who share their unique traits and values. Of course, for far too many people—especially those dealing with traumas including racism, discrimination, poverty, homelessness, addiction, violence, and homophobia/transphobia—therapy is still not covered by their health insurance or is not affordable. Now more than ever, we need to ensure that mental health services are available and accessible to everyone.

Dating coaches will often say that it's impossible to love others without first loving yourself, but Dr. Anhalt is quick to point out that "we can't love ourselves in isolation. Before you can love, you're loved first. But if you weren't loved the way you needed to be, especially when you were a kid, it's often our friends who give us our first taste of what it's like to be loved."

In other words, practicing emotional fitness can teach us how to love ourselves, be more open, and share our needs. "The more we know about ourselves, the more we can understand about why we're attracted to certain people and pulled to certain types of relationships, the more we can see which of those relationships are actually serving us," says Dr. Anhalt.

Looking to learn more about how you show up in your relationships? Take a baby step. Start by practicing one of Dr. Anhalt's excellent emotional fitness tips: do a weekly relationship retrospective with your partner, a coworker, or a close friend. Take turns sharing answers to these three prompts:

*I appreciated / you showed up for me / I felt understood when . . .*
*I felt dropped / I found myself worrying / I felt frustrated when . . .*
*One way we can support each other next week is . . .*

# LOSE THE AGENDA

Sharing food and conversation with strangers can be incredibly powerful. My friend Raman Frey started Good People, a community built around meaningful conversations and delicious feasts for those who value authenticity and connecting without a preconceived agenda. As Raman says, "Who are good people? They're our best selves, when we rise above tribalism and explore big ideas."

Raman has produced more than 250 Good People dinners over the past eight years. Recent dinners have included conversations on costumes and identity, community building, climate change, modern masculinity, systems change, and the arts. Each meal is cooked by a local chef, features a guest speaker, and allows time for small group discussion.

Raman believes that friendship is not an on-demand tap but a *reciprocal intention*. I love that distinction, and it makes me realize that I spend too much time worrying about what there is to gain from hanging out with someone or going to an event. We ask ourselves, "How will this person help my career? Will this dinner be worth my time?" So often we decide where we'll go or who we're going to talk with based on what we think we can gain from that relationship—our interactions are rooted in self-interest. What if we instead built relationships out of mutual curiosity and wonder? What if every person we met had the power to change our life, not because of their job title but because of their unique experience?

"What matters is reciprocal love, respect, and attentiveness," Raman told me. "Friendship is what happens when you stop keeping track of who did what and who owes whom. Friendship might be easier if you share values with someone, but it might be far more rewarding when you don't. Calm down, pay attention, and lose the agenda."

I am certainly guilty of doing exactly what Raman is talking about. I often find myself at a conference, scanning the room, looking for a person who I know can help me book speaking gigs. I often approach conversations as if they are simply a means to an end.

These days, I'm doing my best to strike up a conversation with the first person who starts talking to me at an event. I drop in fully and enthusiastically. I am curious. I pay attention to the person's story. I don't arrive at a dinner party with an agenda or ledger of items I'm seeking. I double down instead of trading up. I try to live by Raman's principle that everyone has something to teach you.

# COME AS YOU ARE

When I told my friend Jeanine Cerundolo I was writing a book on friendship, right away she told me she wanted to share how she and her best friend, Mike Stone, have sustained their friendship for more than fifteen years, since they met as freshmen in college. I asked Jeanine, "What are the rituals and habits you and Mike practice?"

Jeanine answered, "Ritual actually sounds too forced and official—our friendship is way more organic—it's about showing up consistently. It's about making seeing each other a priority, but by desire and joyful default not by an overt intention that feels effortful."

I love that answer. With all of the things on our plate, even friendship has become a chore these days. What if sustaining friendship is less about work and structure and more about *joy* and *authenticity*?

Jeanine and Mike told me their friendship was born out of a mutual feeling of loneliness while living in New York City. Their friendship felt like an oasis in a sea of millions of busy people running around the big city.

They went on to describe what makes their friendship so effortless:

Jeanine and Mike's sense of joy and ease in connecting comes from telling each other to "come as you are." They each know that they don't have to arrive with bells on, put on a happy face, or wait to be in a "presentable place"; they can support each other through whatever is going on for either or both of them.

Jeanine and Mike believe that no matter what they are doing, it's better together, and they make anything fun—for example: trying to hitchhike in France in the rain and making up a song as they went, or moving Jeanine out of her dorm all day and night 'til 3 a.m. They find joy in the companionship itself; and when one is down, the other can help them feel up.

Jeanine and Mike allow each other to be human. They could be having the worst day, but spending time together makes it better. They respect each other thoroughly, honor each other's emotions, and allow each other to be authentic. Their friendship thrives on that.

Jeanine and Mike share their "ongoingnesshood"—the "in the middle of life stuff"—together, not simply catch-ups or updates on independent lives.

Jeanine and Mike have the ability to be comfortable in silence together and not be pressured to make small talk.

Jeanine and Mike believe in each other. They are each other's cheerleaders. But they can also call each other out.

Jeanine and Mike feel comfortable sharing their successes without fearing jealousy, and just as easily sharing failures, too, knowing they'll be understood and uplifted.

Jeanine and Mike laugh together—a lot—there is tons of joy.

Jeanine and Mike don't feel the need to censor themselves or walk on eggshells.

Jeanine and Mike balance sharing feedback or opinions about tough stuff so that it doesn't come across as micromanaging or harsh, but they can have real talk while being kind, gentle, and direct.

In other words, Jeanine and Mike's friendship is understood as a **safe space of mutual trust** that is naturally a place you know you can come to in any state.

Jeanine and Mike teach us that friendship is less about designing the perfect friend date and much more about being with a companion who allows you to feel safe and vulnerable to discuss the "in-between moments" of life. As Aristotle said, "Friendship is the art of holding up a mirror to each other's souls."

With Facebook and Instagram, we're so focused on the highlight moments (getting a new job, traveling somewhere beautiful, falling in love, having children), that catch-ups with friends are often spent rehashing celebratory moments you've already shared online. Instead, take a tip from Jeanine and Mike: create space in your friendship to come as you are—to discuss whatever isn't easy and whatever just *is*.

*Create space in your friendship to come as you are—to discuss whatever isn't easy and whatever just is.*

# DO AN EMOTIONAL BANDWIDTH CHECK

---

Have you ever started talking to a friend about a really emotional subject, only to realize they are emotionally exhausted and don't have the bandwidth to talk about what you want to discuss? This can be really frustrating. My friend Evan Kleiman, aka Bubbles (the Sheriff of Good Times!), once told me about a tool he uses with his partner, Abbie, that I found very helpful. He calls it the emotional bandwidth (EB) check. Whenever Evan and Abbie are about to have an important conversation, they let each other know where their emotional bandwidth is on a scale of one to ten. One means "I haven't had anything to eat today, I was in traffic for an hour, my boss yelled at me, and I can't even decide what I want to eat for dinner (and can you cook dinner for me?)." Ten means "I'm available right now, I have a lot of space right now, and I'm ready to talk about whatever you want to talk about, even the fact that our rent is going up and we need to find a new place to live."

Next time you're looking to have a deep, important conversation with a friend you love, do an EB check—you'll be able to gauge whether your friend is truly able to listen and provide the level of energy and communication you need from them in that moment.

# BE A HYPE PERSON

One of my favorite people in the world to spend time with is Christine Lai, because she is a loyal friend who goes to bat for people she cares about. "Most people live by the Golden Rule," Christine once told me. "That's to treat others like you want to be treated—although some people treat themselves like crap. Instead, I live by the Platinum Rule, which is to treat yourself and others like your best self. Sometimes what we need is a boost of confidence or a cheerleader or someone in our corner to believe in our potential, especially when no one else does. The Golden Rule maintains the status quo; the Platinum Rule is an upward spiral."

Christine has hosted more than three hundred dinners around the world and has made more than five hundred introductions on behalf of people in her network. Since Christine travels so much (she calls herself a "geo-flexible cross-sector collaboration catalyst"), these dinners are an opportunity to bring people she loves and friends of friends together to accelerate serendipity. I recently asked Christine how she manages to have close relationships with so many people. "Follow through," she said. "If Smiley comes up in my brain, it's up to me to follow through, reach out, and set up a time to hang out with Smiley."

If you want to hang out with someone, don't wait for the person to call you. Be proactive and make it happen.

Christine is so good at introductions that by the time you get home from meeting with her, she's already made two introductions on your behalf and they're waiting for you in your inbox. Shit, sometimes Christine has connected me to someone I didn't even remember us talking about! Contrast this to my usual MO—I tell someone I'm going to make an intro for them to an important professional contact, but don't send the email for six weeks.

Here are a few tips to keep in mind when making introductions for your friends:

**Get the double opt-in.** Always ask permission before clogging someone's inbox and requesting their time or wisdom and/or connecting them with a stranger.

**Follow through.** If you say you're going to connect someone, do it and do it in a timely manner.

**Keep it simple.** One or two sentences is fine. Include links to each person's website or LinkedIn to make it easy for your friends.

**Provide context.** Why are you making this intro? What's the mutual interest or ask?

**Be a hype person.** Making your friends look good makes you look good, too.

Here's an example from an introduction Christine made for me just the other day:

Hi Roya and Smiley,

Hope your week is off to a stellar start!

In follow-up to communication with you both, excited to make this e-introduction (Roya—Smiley, Smiley—Roya).

Roya, Smiley [with a hyperlink to my website] is a dear friend who is an author and speaker. As you shared some of the things you're working on, I immediately thought of Smiley because of the work he's done with the Women's Speaker Initiative.

Smiley, Roya [with a hyperlink to Roya's website] is a new friend I met last night at a community potluck. She currently works with the Galvanize community and has been aggregating events to share with women speakers. Some clear alignment, and hopeful opportunities, to connect some dots!

Tag-teaming you two to take it from here. If there is anything I can do to be of assistance, please let me know.

Take care and have a wonderful week,
Roya and Smiley!

# HAVE A CLOSET OF
# TRUST AT WORK

Work friendships are becoming more and more rare as more and more organizations have distributed workforces, shifted to working remotely, and use technology (instead of in-person meetings) for communication. At the same time, workplace burnout is skyrocketing: 70 percent of millennials experience burnout and 30 percent say they are always or often burned out at work. The World Health Organization has even redefined *burnout* as a syndrome linked to chronic stress at work.

We've been taught that work isn't a place to be friends with people— it's a place to get work done. According to Dan Schawbel, connection expert and author of *Back to Human*, the workplace is becoming more disconnected than ever before, and 10 percent of people have zero friends at work. Dan notes that while technology can be a powerful collaboration tool to bring people together across geographic boundaries, it's important that, once we're in the same room, we turn off our phones so we can actually connect and learn from each other.

One friend of mine was able to cultivate close friendships at work by having a closet of trust (aka "the COT") with three of her coworkers. My friend and her colleagues, who are all public schoolteachers, started with a three-way group chat on Messenger, where they sent pictures and comments and vented about frustrating things at work. Then, they started meeting in a three-by-ten-foot closet at the office, where they could share freely about what was going on. Yes, their safe space is an actual closet! "What happens in the closet of trust stays in the closet of trust," she told me. "It's the only thing that gets me through the day."

In *The Business of Friendship*, Shasta Nelson shows that friendships at work benefit us with greater happiness, health, and job satisfaction, and the best employees are those who have a best friend at work. "Our goal is for more of us to 'feel seen in safe and satisfying ways' by those with whom we're spending most of our time interacting: our coworkers," she says.

Find one or two people at work who you trust. Then find a safe, secret place to talk at work—maybe it's a closet, a conference room, the stairwell, a coffee shop nearby, or a group text thread—where you feel permitted to vent about what's going on, so you can support each other at work.

We spend a third of our waking lives working. Building meaningful relationships with the people you work with will help you become a more engaged employee—and a more fulfilled human.

# START SAYING NO

I think the main difference between your twenties and your thirties is that in your twenties, you say yes to everything people ask you to do.

Want to come to happy hour on Wednesday after work? "Sure!"

Want to go out for drinks tonight? "Ahhh, I'm tired of drinking, but yeah, I'll spend money on feeling terrible tomorrow."

Brunch?! "Yeah, I'll drop twenty-three dollars on eggs that I can cook myself at home, whatever."

Sunday night, want to come to my place for movie night? "Uhhhh, I'm in my sweatpants and really don't want to get in the car, but yeaaaaah, I'll be over in an hour."

Growing up means saying, "No, I'm good," to things your friends want you to do, even if those things are really cool and enticing. Growing up means sometimes you stay in on Friday night and go to bed at 9 p.m. because that's exactly what you want to do.

Real friendship isn't doing everything your friends ask of you; real friendship is honesty and taking care of your needs first. Saying *no* more often will help you say *yes* to the things—and the people—that matter most.

# BE LESS FLAKY

I grew up on the East Coast, so I have a particular revulsion to how most people on the West Coast make plans. On the East Coast, if you want to hang out with someone, and they want to hang out with you, you simply say, "Cool, let's hang out next Saturday!" And it's done.

On the West Coast, if you want to hang out with someone, you likely will have no idea whether they actually want to hang out with you or they are just saying they want to hang out with you, because they can't commit to a specific time to see you, and you will bump into each other for six months without actually ever making a formal plan to hang out.

Here's how the conversation goes down in the Bay Area, where I've lived for almost ten years.

**Me:** "Hey, friend! It has been forever. You look great. It's good to see you!"

**Friend:** "Hey, Smiley! Oh my god! Good to see you, too! I know, we need to catch up sometime!"

**Me:** "Yes, we do! I miss you!"

**Friend:** "Oh my god, I miss you, too!"

**Me:** "Cool, how about we hang out next Saturday?"

**Friend:** "Ummm, next Saturday?"

**Me:** "Yeah, next Saturday! Let's make a plan now so we're confirmed."

**Friend:** "Ummmm, yeah, ummmm."

**Me:** "Are you busy next Saturday?"

**Friend:** "Ummmm, I'm not sure."

**Me:** "Do you want to check your calendar?"

**Friend:** "Ummmm, I'm not sure."

**Me:** "Your calendar is on your phone, yes? Your phone is in your pocket, yes?"

**Friend:** "Ummmm, I'm just, I'm not sure about next Saturday. How about we play it by ear and check in next week?"

**Me:** "Well, you said that the last time I bumped into you. How about we make a plan right now? Does the Saturday after next work for you?"

**Friend:** "Two Saturdays from now?"

**Me:** "Yes."

**Friend:** "Ummm, I'm not sure. How about we play it by ear and check in in two weeks?"

Here's the deal. If you care about someone, you have to carve out time and space to be with them. Plain and simple. If you don't want to spend time with someone—or you have other people and projects that are higher priority right now—let them know the truth. There is nothing worse than faking that you want to spend time with someone when you really don't want to.

Try this:

*"It's really nice to bump into you, Friend! Right now, I'm spending most of my energy focused on [whatever you're focused on], and I can't make a plan, but I'll reach out in a few months when I have more space."*

Being less flaky will help you gain clarity on what matters most in your life. You'll start cultivating relationships with people who honor their commitments. Instead of focusing on flakers, you'll be genuinely excited about how you're spending your time and who you're spending your time with.

# PART THREE

# Invest in Friendship

# START SLOW

There have been times when I've gone to an hour-long networking event and by the time the event is over, the organizer has claimed that everyone is now best friends. So, apparently I have one hundred new friends... but I don't really know a single one of them. I find this practice annoying and also destructive to our goal of being more intentional about friendship. It's great to attend a lot of events and work on building your community, but just because you and someone else are in the same room doesn't mean you instantly owe them anything.

Friendship takes time. It's like "We've only spent an hour together. I barely know you. It was nice meeting you and eating kale salad with you, and maybe we'll hang out sometime again, but no, we're not best friends—or even *friends*—yet."

My friend Eva recommends practicing the "slow-build friendship." This means that if you meet someone who seems cool, instead of coming on too strong, build the friendship slowly. Ask them if they want to go for a walk sometime or plan to hang out. Invite them to a fun event. Send them an article they might like.

As you spend more time together, hopefully the friendship flame begins to burn a little stronger. In one of her SuperSoul Sessions, Brené

Brown offers the useful analogy of a jar full of marbles to explain what it means to build trust between two people. Each time you add a marble, you're building the relationship's container of trust. You can only fill the jar of marbles by having many small moments of kindness and intimacy and shared experience over time.

In fact, research by Jeffery A. Hall, associate professor of communications studies at the University of Kansas, suggests that you need to spend at least ninety hours with someone before they consider you a real friend. His study found that it usually takes about fifty hours of time together to go from acquaintance to casual friend, around ninety hours to become a true friend, and more than two hundred hours to be close friends and feel an emotional connection with someone.

Trust can't happen overnight, and neither can friendship.

# ALWAYS GO ON
# A SECOND DATE

---

It's hard enough to meet cool people, but what do you do when you've met someone really cool and want to keep the friendship momentum going? With dating, if a first date goes well, you ask them on a second date. If you have a nice conversation over dinner, maybe you make a plan to go to a movie or see a show. How does that work for friendship? Do you just keep asking them to dinner over and over again?

My friend Sahar Massachi, a data and software engineer, digital campaign builder, and community organizer, is one of the most socially active people I know. Sahar believes that friend momentum starts with sharing your intention up front. "I have a friendship card instead of a business card," he explains. On one side it says, *Let's be friends*, and on the other is his email and phone number and the phrase *Write code, defeat evil*. "Giving someone my information is less stress on my end," says Sahar. "If they want to see me, too, they have to take the initiative and call."

Whenever Sahar meets someone interesting, he gives them his friendship card. He also has an event already on the calendar that he can invite them to: Every month he schedules a picnic in the park or a potluck dinner over the span of a few hours, and he invites all the new people he met in the previous month and his existing friends. This way, whenever he meets someone new who he wants to bring into his circle, he has a second date already in motion. Not only that, but he creates opportunities for his new connections to become friends with his other friends, creating new bonds and possibilities for collaboration.

Sahar's approach mirrors advice from psychologist and friendship expert Dr. Marisa Franco, who told me that repetition is an important way to make new friends. "It's not just about getting out there," she says. "It's about getting out there repeatedly to the same event or group." This practice reflects a psychological principle known as the *mere-exposure effect*, which reveals that the more we see someone, the more we like them. This is why Dr. Franco recommends signing up for ongoing activities like a book club, improv group, or language class (or a monthly potluck dinner hosted by Sahar) more than going out to a bar or a one-off event. The repeated interactions you have with other attendees at those gatherings can lead to fruitful friendships.

The desire to connect people offline has translated into how Sahar shows up online as well. Sahar will often make "Job Yenta" posts on Facebook, putting a call out to see who in his network is looking for a job and who is hiring. He even turned Yenta into a newsletter and brought on a team of volunteers to cull through the spreadsheet of responses, looking to match people looking for work with job offers, as well as people looking for housing with those looking for roommates, and single friends with other single friends looking for romance.

"It's hard to know who my real friends are," Sahar told me. "It's very hard for me to have a core group of friends that remains the same as I move across time and distance. For me, friendship happens when you know you'll see the person again in the future. I want to create that regular heartbeat so that community can thrive."

The last time Sahar and I hung out, we took a stroll down Valencia Street in the Mission and walked into one of my favorite independent bookstores, Dog Eared Books. Sahar asked, "Do you want to do a book swap?" I was like, "What's that?" "It's when I buy you a book I think you would like, and you buy me a book you think I would like," he replied.

I had never heard of a book swap before, but I loved it. Instead of just walking into a bookstore and telling your buddy what they should read, what a beautiful idea to give them something right then and there. The cashier rang us up, remarking, "You two are really sweet," and we both walked out of the bookstore with gifts in our hand. It made my weekend.

I asked Sahar for his favorite piece of friendship advice. "Organize," he said. "I've met so many amazing people because of activism and organizing. Being in the struggle for liberation is good for the soul. It teaches you how to be accountable to someone. How to be with others. How to disagree. How to work with others toward a common goal. The world is all kinds of corrupted, and fighting back is good for you. Keeping in mind your vision for the future is an important part of being a human being."

# GO DEEP RATHER
# THAN WIDE

---

Meeting new people is important, especially when you move to a new city or are looking to expand your social circle, but one of my goals for this year was to spend more time going deep with the close friends I already have and less time investing energy in new relationships. I wanted to simplify things, choosing depth over breadth.

Since 2012—the year I moved to San Francisco—I've been so active in my communities that I often feel overwhelmed trying to maintain dozens of casual surface-level relationships. During the pandemic, I felt like I only had bandwidth for my closest friends. This mirrors the conclusion reached in Lifeboat's *State of Friendship in America* report, which found that close friends are the ones that matter most. "It's not about the number of people you associate with. It's about the quality of those relationships," the report stated. Participants said they would prefer deeper friendships over sheer numbers by more than two to one, and this proportion holds across demographic groups like age, gender, geography, and political leanings.

According to Shasta Nelson, a former pastor turned friendship expert, there are three things we must practice in order to increase intimacy in our friendships: positivity, consistency, and vulnerability. In her book *Frientimacy*, Shasta shares that to feel satisfied with our friends, we need to practice *positivity* with each other. To feel safe, we need to practice *consistency* with each other. And to feel seen, we need to practice being *vulnerable* with each other.

One of my favorite people to go deep with is my friend Kelly McFarling. Kelly and I met in college, and she's an incredibly talented musician. Kelly and I don't get to see each other frequently. Kelly is on tour playing shows across the country, and I'm on the road speaking; but when we're both in town, we'll have what Kelly calls a "deep hang." Deep hangs are when you're able to catch up right where you left off with someone you truly care about; you don't even miss a beat, even if you haven't seen them in six months or a year.

On a recent deep hang with Kelly, I drove up to Bolinas, California, and we kicked it at a cabin in the woods. We went for a walk in the rain with her dogs, we cooked dinner by candlelight because the power went out, we had a sleepover, and then we made breakfast in the morning. My deep hang with Kelly met all three of Shasta's requirements for cultivating frientimacy. It was exciting, joyful, and *positive*; we spent most of the day laughing. We felt safe because we had been intentional and *consistent* about getting together. We also felt seen because we spent a lot of time sharing *vulnerably* about what was really going on in our lives.

Here are five habits to keep in mind when planning a deep hang with a close friend:

**1. Presence.** Put away the phone and really just *be* with your friend. One of my favorite things about having deep hangs with my friends who have children is that you have to pay attention when you're playing with little kids. You can't take your eyes off them or start scrolling through cat videos.

**2. Don't double book.** There's nothing worse than having a deep hang that has to be cut short because you made plans to go to an event that you don't even want to go to. If you're having a deep hang, clear the calendar for the whole day to allow for spontaneity.

**3. Be intentional about place.** Deep hangs should include adventures to beautiful spaces and places. A waterfall, the beach, a secret garden, a mini road trip, an Airbnb out of town; all of these are more exciting venues than your local coffee shop. Challenge yourself to design an experience that you want to share with someone special.

**4. Plan a sleepover.** Remember how fun sleepovers were when you were a kid? You got all that time together to eat popcorn, debate which movie to watch, laugh out loud gossiping before bed, and make pancakes for breakfast. We need more platonic adult sleepovers! Next time you have a deep hang, plan a sleepover with your close friend so you have much more time to play.

**5. Get past the highlights.** It's easy to ask questions about things you've already seen on a friend's Instagram feed. "OMG, how was Mexico?!" Instead, ask what's going on in your friend's love life, or how their family is doing, or what's something they are struggling with, or what their goals are for next year.

# HONOR THE ONE-ON-ONE

Have you ever shown up excited to see a friend you haven't seen in a while, only to get to dinner and realize that your friend has invited another friend to dinner as well? Your friend will say, "I was talking to Rachel and realized she didn't have plans tonight, so I invited her to join us because I thought you two would get along anyway. Yay!"

This is the worst. When you make a plan with one person, honor the one-on-one. This will lead to a more intimate conversation and give you the time and space to go deep and really catch up. If you invite a third person, you'll spend half the conversation just bringing them up to speed, catching them up on life events and inside jokes.

Every year, my friend Logan makes a New Year's resolution to go on one-on-one overnight trips with at least five different friends as a way to go deeper with her favorite people. "If you just meet up with an old friend for a few hours, you spend the whole time catching up," she explains. "But when you go away together, you get through all of that stuff early on, and then you can actually talk about life. By day two and three, you're getting to the really good stuff, the stuff that you just wouldn't talk about over brunch." This reminds me of Sherry Turkle's words in her book *Reclaiming Conversation*: "A face-to-face

*The best friendships
are ones that have space
to grow on their own.*

conversation is the most human—and humanizing—thing we do. Fully present to one another, we learn to listen. It's where we develop the capacity for empathy. It's where we experience the joy of being heard, of being understood."

When you're in college, you want everyone to be friends with each other. I have fond memories of strolling around campus, inviting every single person I saw to come to the same party. When you get older, you realize that not everyone has to be friends and that your friends don't all have to like each other. The best friendships are ones that have space to grow on their own. Commit to the one-on-one; it will lead to intimacy, depth, and growth in your relationships.

# KNOW WHO'S IN YOUR CIRCLE

In life before Facebook (L.B.F.), it was a lot easier to know who your real friends were. Facebook makes it harder to distinguish between the people you truly love—the people you know are going to be part of your life as you grow older—and people you just met last week. Everyone is just a tiny avatar with their headshot. But we all know that not all friends are created equal. As community building expert Casper ter Kuile says, "We need to know who's bringing the birthday cake to the party. Who are my five people?!"

My friend Lauren Weinstein recommends making a visual representation of your friends called a Friend Circle. In a Friend Circle, you draw concentric circles around yourself. Each circle represents a level of intimacy for the people in your life.

In the very first circle are your family of origin or family of choice.

In the second circle are your best friends who feel like family. Lauren calls this circle Tier 1. Your dearest friends. Your ride or dies. The people who would be your bridesmaids or groomsmen if you were to have those at your wedding. The people you can turn to when you are sick.

In the third circle (Tier 2) are your close friends. The people you feel close to and connected to and know what's happening in their lives, but the communication is less frequent than your Tier 1s.

In the fourth and outermost circle (Tier 3) are friends in your extended network. Really good people you've spent time with over the years. You have a special connection, and it feels really good to see them every now and then when you're in their city or hosting a house party, but you're not in touch with them regularly. I like how Lauren divides this fourth ring of the circle by geographic location and experiences (college, study abroad, different cities, different jobs, etc.). These are her communities from all the places she's lived and the experiences she's had.

*Note:* Pay attention to which people don't make your outer Tier 3 circle. It's not to say that these people suck or don't matter to you, just that they aren't someone you are prioritizing right now. On the backside of the sheet of paper where I made my Friend Circle, I actually wrote a list of people who aren't in my outer circle but I still think are good people who I want to keep in my orbit and stay abreast of, even if we don't ever talk. I call it my Cool Humans list. These are nice people I've met along the way, attended a conference or community event with, or people I've connected with over social media or through mutual friends. I'm glad these Cool Humans exist, but I don't know them very well, and I'm okay with the fact that we're not ever going to be close friends. I'm grateful that we had the opportunity to connect a few times in this lifetime, and I wish them only the best.

Making a Friend Circle is a useful exercise to determine which friendships you should be investing in. If you feel like you don't have any Tier 1 friends, that might be a sign you need to go deeper with someone you really like spending time with. If you're prioritizing someone as a Tier 1 friend and they don't think of you as a close friend, then clearly there's some misalignment and you need to talk about your friendship.

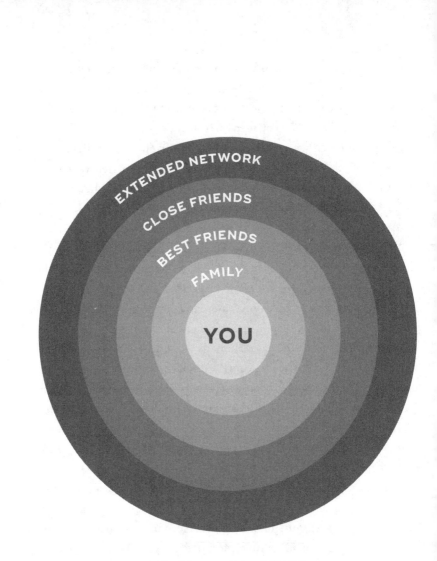

EXTENDED NETWORK

CLOSE FRIENDS

BEST FRIENDS

FAMILY

YOU

Who's in your Friend Circle?

# HAVE FEWER
# FACEBOOK FRIENDS

I first joined Facebook when I was living abroad in Buenos Aires, Argentina, in 2008. I remember thinking it was weird when I met new people at a bar and they would ask me, "Do you have Facebook? Let's be friends!" The good thing is that, more than ten years later, I can keep track of all these people who live in Argentina, thousands of miles away, now that I don't live there anymore. On the other hand, I have dozens of Facebook friends I've only met once at a bar—in other words, I'm "friends" with people who aren't really friends of mine.

Anthropological research suggests that the human brain's limited capacity can actually only maintain relationships with fewer than 150 people. This principle is often called Dunbar's number, first proposed long before Facebook (or MySpace!) (or Friendster!!), in the 1990s, by British anthropologist Robin Dunbar. He explained it as "the number of people you would not feel embarrassed about joining uninvited for a drink if you happened to bump into them in a bar."

Some would say that 150 people is still too many to form a deep relationship; research has shown that strong bonds tend to occur in what psychologists refer to as "sympathy groups" of 10 to 15 people. Today, some of us are connected to hundreds or even thousands of people—

like me and my 4,867 Facebook friends. How the hell am I supposed to maintain relationships with that many people?! Clearly, I'm not. Perhaps the number of Facebook friends I have is less of an indication of the quality of my social relationships and more an indication of how much time I spend posting on Facebook.

Making a Friend Circle helped Lauren Weinstein figure out who she wanted to be close with and who was important to her. She realized that having people in her Facebook feed she wasn't close with (a) diluted the power of her actual connections, (b) helped her realize that many of her Facebook connections were people she had friended purely for networking purposes, and (c) helped her clarify who she wanted to actually spend time with in real life, not on Facebook.

For a while, Lauren used the "If I ran into this person IRL, would I want to have a conversation?" question as a litmus test for whether she would add or accept them as friends on Facebook. She would sign onto Facebook and see someone in her feed, and wonder, *Who the heck is this person?* She recalls that one time she actually did run into the person IRL, and after they didn't even stop to say hi, she unfriended them.

Lauren's rule was "If I ran into them in a city, would we hang? Or would I want to have a convo with them? As Facebook popped up birthday reminders, it was a way to ask myself, are we even friends? Would I even want to wish this person a happy birthday?!"

Lauren told me that she checks Facebook occasionally, but the value of Facebook has decreased to her personally. "Maybe it's because I'm more assured of my friendships and my place in the world, and I don't need to accept people just to have a large network on Facebook for a job," she shares. "And, because I value the personal connection, Facebook has become less important to me to track all the connections I've made over the years in my work and travels."

I've had a similar experience to Lauren in the past year. The more I've become clear on the people who matter most to me, the more secure about who I am in the world, the less value I've placed on Facebook's relevance in my life. From obsessing over the number of likes a post gets, to scrutinizing the number of friends I have, to scrolling through a news feed of "friends" I don't even know—it all starts to feel like a giant waste of time.

# TREAT YOUR FRIENDS

When you go out to dinner, do you split the check or does one person treat? I used to be a splitter. It seemed like the fairest way to ensure no one got stuck with a large bill. I was such a splitter that not only did I make sure my friends and I split the check, but if one friend ordered something more expensive—or ordered two drinks when I only had one—I made sure they put in extra on the bill. This was awkward as hell and also caused me great anxiety every time a check came.

Several friends have taught me that you experience more joy when you take turns buying someone you love a meal. For example, every few months, Christine and I go out for lunch to catch up on all things life, work, and love. It's our friendship deep-dive, where we get to see each other, ask each other hard questions, and hold each other accountable for anything we mentioned we were working on during our last meal. We always go somewhere delicious to eat, and we always take turns paying. The main reason I love this is that it keeps our deep-dives going—there's always another meal to look forward to because we each want to return the favor next time (and on and on it goes). In addition, it feels really good when your friend is treating you to a meal and perhaps even better when you treat someone you care about to a meal.

If you're not in a financial position to cover your friend, let them know. My buddy Ryan and I used to determine who would cover our meetings over coffee and bagels with lox based on who was "holding" at the time. When I met Ryan, I was unemployed. Even though Ryan was a freelance journalist, refereeing dodgeball to help pay the bills, he still covered me most of the time since he was "holding" and I was broke. Fast-forward a few years, and I started treated Ryan—unless he had just published a big piece—in which case, he was so pumped, he paid for me. This beats splitting the check every time you go out.

Treat your friends. It will lead to gratitude and intimacy.

# DON'T ASK. JUST HELP.

One of my friends recently began treatment for a rare form of cancer, and I told her partner, "Let me know what I can do to help! I'd be happy to make a meal or pick up anything if you guys need an extra hand." Not surprisingly, my friend said thanks, but never reached out to ask me to help. Sometimes being a good friend means helping out before you're even asked for help.

My friend Dr. Emily Anhalt, a clinical psychologist and mental health expert, who I mentioned earlier, recently shared this emotional fitness tip for any relationship: "'Let me know what I can do . . .' is well-intentioned but not helpful. Do the extra four minutes of work to think of something that would be helpful, and then do it."

She then offered a few suggestions:

For a stressed colleague: leave their favorite lunch on their desk on a day when they probably won't have time to go out and get food.

For a fund-raising founder: reach out to a few investors who might be interested and ask if you can make an intro. Then make it.

For a friend going through a tough time: have a gift basket delivered with easy-to-enjoy treats.

For a new mom: find out what kind of diapers she uses and have a box delivered.

For anyone at all: ask them, at a time when all is well, how they like to be treated or supported when they're down. Take note and refer back to that when needed.

After reviewing Emily's suggestion, I ordered several bottles of my friend's favorite kombucha and had them delivered to her apartment while she was recovering from surgery. It's a small thing, but my friend knew I was there to support her.

# EXCHANGE YOUR TALENTS

At the end of 2018, I really beat myself up focusing on all the things that weren't working in my life. I criticized myself for being thirty-five and living with roommates, for watching *Love Actually* for like the eleventh year in a row *still* single, and approaching my love life from a place of lack. That's when my friend Vika Viktoria suggested we start a talent exchange. "What if I helped you navigate love and relationships?" Vika asked. "I want to offer you my relationship coaching practice for free, since you've been so generous with your time helping advise me with my speaking business."

I decided to take Vika's offer seriously. I met her at her apartment in Santa Monica, and she helped me design self-love practices, challenge my limiting beliefs around why I'm still single, and get closer to my personal values and the values I'm looking for in a partner. She helped me stand in my power. She helped me realize that my creative lifestyle attracts my partner; that I create time for what matters to me; that I am ready to be challenged and inspired by my partner; that I am a loving, kind, handsome, funny, interesting, joyful, creative, sensual, and devoted man; and that there is an amazing woman out there for me and I'm so excited to meet her!

She even led me on an hour-long visioning meditation over the phone, where I wrote a love letter to my future partner. She told me that I should put it under my pillow, and then someday in the future, after I've met the love of my life, I'll give her the letter and say, "I dreamed about you and wrote you this letter a long time ago."

Vika and I have continued to chat over the phone every month or so. One month is a speaker coaching call for Vika to share the progress she's making on growing her speaking business on the power of storytelling and intersectional masculinity; I offer advice on building her website, booking more gigs, and positioning herself in the speaking industry. The next month we check in about my love life, my relationship, and how my heart is doing. It's a talent exchange built on mutual admiration and a shared interest in personal and professional purpose.

Vika recently sent me this text message: "Smiley—I am so grateful to you. You filled me up with wind in my sails, encouraging me forward and guiding me to clearer seas. I feel immensely grateful for our friendship; the kind that educates and inspires, uplifts and emboldens us in the direction of our dreams. I'm always here for you and so proud of the incredible moves you're making from the heart, for the heart. Keep shining, Vika."

Sometimes we need someone to put the wind in our sails; a friendtor, not just a friend. Think about someone in your life you can support right now with your talents and skills. And I should note: Your talent exchange doesn't have to be a one-for-one exchange. Just because you help someone design a website, write a business plan, file their taxes, or decorate their bedroom doesn't mean they need to help you right away. Just because you offer one hour of your time doesn't mean they need to offer one hour of their time.

One of my favorite rituals to facilitate connection in a physical space is to set up a Needs and Gives wall. On a Needs and Gives wall, everyone gets a piece of paper and on that paper they share three things they are seeking and three things they are willing to offer the group. Everyone puts their sheet of paper on a large wall, with their name and contact info, so folks can see the expertise and potential available without even leaving the room. Needs and offers might be professional things like a new job, start-up capital, or a new website. Or, they might be more personal things like self-care, finding a new apartment, or home gardening tips.

During the pandemic, we did a Needs and Gives exercise in my Author Support Group, a five-week course I led on Zoom for authors writing their books during quarantine. Because we didn't have a physical wall, we used a Google spreadsheet. Everyone wrote three things they needed for the book they were writing and three things they were willing to offer to the sixty other authors in the group. Immediately, authors looking for publications to which they could pitch articles found them.

This isn't tit for tat; it's about sharing your gifts with the people you want to help succeed. It's about creating a reciprocal cycle of mentorship among friends. All too often we seek answers to our questions externally. We search online for hours to find expert advice, but we forget to ask people in the same room (or Zoom) as us if they'd be willing to help us. Of course, you have to be excited about the talent exchange or this won't work. If you don't feel comfortable helping someone, then definitely don't agree to help. Remember the power of saying *no*. Research by Adam Grant, organizational psychologist, Wharton professor, and author of *Give and Take*, has shown that *givers who are intentional with their time* are much more successful in life than takers who are just out for themselves, matchers who only pursue fair exchanges, or over-givers who say *yes* to every opportunity thrown their way.

# GET SOMEBODY ELSE A GIG

Noble Prize–winning novelist Toni Morrison once said, "Just remember that your real job is that if you are free, you need to free somebody else. If you have some power, then your job is to empower somebody else."

I've tried to live by these words as much as possible, knowing that the work of co-liberation will never be over. As I started speaking at more and more companies and conferences around the world, it became very clear the majority of other speakers onstage were like me. In other words, they were white men—usually much older white men than me—but still, all too often, keynote speakers were cis-gender, white, and male. Furthermore, I was disheartened (but not surprised) to find out that many events I had spoken at or attended were paying female speakers and speakers of color less than white male speakers with similar levels of experience.

In one case, I co-emceed an event with my friend—a woman of color—and was paid several thousand dollars for the gig while she was paid nothing. This event wasn't run by some evil large corporation, either. It was run by a purpose-driven leadership conference that claimed to be a champion of social justice. In that case, I said something, and the conference ended up paying my friend the same amount they paid me.

This isn't an isolated incident, either. Research shows that women are invited to give fewer talks than men at top US universities, and the gap is even worse for women of color. A University of California, Hastings study found that a full 100 percent of women of color working in STEM fields reported gender bias in their profession. Compared to every dollar that men earn, women earn just eighty cents; and compared to white, non-Hispanic men, Black women make sixty-three cents while Latina women earn only fifty-four cents.

To do something about this, I began investing more time and energy in ensuring that there is equity in the speaking industry I work in. This includes efforts like encouraging event planners to book more Black speakers and speakers of color, ensuring that those speakers and other underrepresented speakers are paid competitively for their work, and encouraging fellow speakers to share resources and opportunities with their colleagues, especially their colleagues from different backgrounds. Since 2017, the Women/Womxn, BIPOC, and Inclusivity Speaker Initiative has grown into an international community of more than 4,000 members and has led to hundreds of speakers getting gigs, increasing their speaking fees, and, most importantly, investing in each other.

Good things happen when we pay it forward.

When you start approaching your career from an abundance mindset, the ripples of impact never end. As Lynne Twist, cofounder of the Pachamama Alliance and founder of the Soul of Money Institute says, "What you appreciate, appreciates."

# REPAIR WHAT'S BROKEN

As with entering an adult friendship, there is very little agreed upon protocol for how to *mend* or *end* an adult friendship. Do you acknowledge that you've drifted apart from someone and specify that you don't want to be friends anymore? Or do you decide not to say anything and let time speak for itself—the friendship equivalent of being ghosted by a Bumble date?

My friend Logan Ury, a dating coach and director of relationship science at the dating app Hinge, reminded me that it's okay for friendships to ebb and flow. It's okay to take a break and reset your friend expectations. "You don't have to cut anyone off," Logan said.

Maybe the person will come back in a new season of your life when you least expect it. If you cut off a friend, you are cutting off a potential opportunity. Unlike in dating, where dating someone you feel "meh" about for five years will likely keep you for five years from meeting someone you feel better about, there's less of a downside from not firing your friends. After all, you never know when you're going to move to a random city and that old friend is going to be the only person you know who lives there.

Logan offers the unusual practice of breakup consulting. An individual will come to her to discuss whether or not they should break up with their partner. Logan helps that person think through this decision. If the person decides to move forward with it, they come up with a plan for making the breakup as intentional and respectful as possible. Logan coaches the person through the breakup conversation, holds them accountable for actually *doing* the breaking up, and guides them through the painful post-breakup period.

Sometimes one of Logan's breakup consulting clients decides to stay in the relationship and reinvest.

While it might feel tempting to dump a friend who has wronged you, it's first worth considering whether you want to trade in your breakup plan for a reconnection plan. In a reconnection plan, two friends might tell each other what isn't working, take responsibility for where they've failed to show up for each other, and discuss how they are willing to change in order to mend the friendship. Or perhaps they decide the friendship isn't serving them right now and wish to take a break. This process certainly will require more time and energy but will likely make you feel better than ghosting.

If you feel a friend has hurt you or isn't healthy for you anymore or you want to take a break from them, it's important to let them know. Getting something heavy off your chest can be liberating. Repairing relationships and being in integrity is good for you. Take inspiration from two experts on friendship, Aminatou Sow and Ann Friedman, who cowrote the book *Big Friendship*, host the podcast *Call Your Girlfriend*, and have been best friends and coworkers for many years. Aminatou and Ann decided to go to couples therapy together when things weren't working in their (platonic) relationship.

As Aminatou recalls, "We were just at an impasse, where we were in this cycle, where for a year or more, we were both trying to come back to the friendship that we had in the beginning, and it just was not working. I was really frustrated with my efforts with Ann. She was really frustrated with her efforts with me. . . . Finally, it was actually a talk about work that led to this, because we were having a lot of difficulties communicating together, and we finally just put it all on the table, and it was like, 'Hi, I don't know how to talk to you and how do we go about doing this?'"

Both Aminatou and Ann wanted to be able to say that they had done *everything* possible to help their relationship, and it turns out that platonic friends can also go to couples therapy—and it's not as wild an idea as it sounds. Therapy wasn't easy, but it helped them communicate clearly, find a common language for their friendship, and learn more about themselves in the process.

My friend Casper ter Kuile, author of *The Power of Ritual* and cofounder of the Sacred Design Lab, a research and design consultancy working to create a culture of belonging, wrote that the hardest thing he did last year was listing the people he felt out of relationship with and finding what the best way back to reconnection was. In some cases, he apologized over the phone. For others, he prayed or meditated.

With each friendship he wanted to repair, Casper, together with his cofounder Angie Thurston, asked himself four questions:

1. *What is the issue as I understand it?*
2. *What is the vision I'd like for the future?*
3. *What action might I take to make that happen?*
4. *What risk might that action involve?*

Casper reflected that in every instance, the reaching out felt massively affirmed and welcomed. In some cases, actual contact was not going to be wise or fruitful, but the reflection process was still helpful. "Though this didn't miraculously wipe everything away and there are still difficult relationships I have and others I will need to repair, I feel more capable [in my relationships] than ever before," he wrote.

In the digital age, we don't think twice about ghosting or swiping left on a potential partner. Perhaps technology has created the illusion that the perfect friend will be right around the corner, just like the perfect Tinder date. But what if nobody is perfect? What if you end up having the same problems with a new friend that you have with your current friend? What if it's really about how you're showing up? It's worth it to have the messy conversations required to repair your relationships. As the English poet David Whyte reminds us, "Without tolerance and mercy all friendships die."

# LIVE IN DEATH'S FACE

A few years ago, my mom retired from being a nurse-practitioner, where she worked at the Veterans Administration (VA) for more than thirty years, helping those who had served in the military and fought in World War II, Vietnam, Iraq, and Afghanistan. Many of her patients suffered from PTSD and other serious health problems. Later in her career, she worked in hospice and palliative care, helping advocate for dignified end-of-life care for veterans and their families.

My mom, a breast cancer survivor, found caring for people at such a vulnerable time in their lives so meaningful that she is still volunteering weekly at the hospice clinic, eight years after retirement. She wanted to ensure that her patients' final days were spent as painlessly and as peacefully as possible in the company of loved ones and not in a hospital surrounded by IV tubes. Even during the pandemic, when visitors were prohibited from visiting their loved ones, my mom made hospice support phone calls, helping families prepare for the death of a loved one.

The truth is that our society is not good at dealing with death. We don't want to talk about it; we want to pretend that it doesn't exist, that it will never happen to us. All too often we wait to ask ourselves important questions about dying until it is too late. My mom is part of a growing movement of people who believe that by creating more space to talk about death, we can become more thoughtful about our choices and how we live.

This is the purpose of one of my favorite communities, You're Going to Die: Poetry, Prose & Everything Goes, an open-mic variety show that features stories, music, and sharing about death and dying. You're Going to Die was started by Ned Buskirk in 2009, in his own apartment in San Francisco that he shared with his wife, as a place to gather friends and build community. Ned had lost his mother to breast cancer and later lost his mother-in-law, and he needed a place to have conversations about loss. He saw You're Going to Die as a space for people to share, listen, laugh, and cry about death.

"My intention behind this event is that we are here to be with death and let death know we are okay with death right now," Ned shared at a You're Going to Die event, not long after his mother-in-law died in 2012. "This is a space to come as close as we can to death and being with it—and also be alive and not be depressing. . . . To live in death's face. To know that death is a powerful source of inspiration. And living well. And loving."

You're Going to Die soon spread from Ned's apartment to small cafés and larger event spaces like the Great American Music Hall, one of San Francisco's most storied concert venues. In 2020, the event marked its ten-year anniversary with a sold-out, 650-person show at the Independent, full of musicians, friends, storytellers, and community members. YG2D is now an official 501c3 nonprofit organization. It supports Alive Inside, a prison program that hosts shows for the incarcerated, allowing a structured open-mic space for those in prison to share stories, poems, and songs about loss and grief while making room for being alive with what we have. It also supports Songs for Life, a free program where musicians offer their talents and companionship for hospice patients and their communities.

Even though You're Going to Die has grown into a movement with 25,000 followers around the world, it still feels like you're being invited into a small, intimate gathering in Ned's home with his closest friends. I remember attending a You're Going to Die event at the Lost Church in San Francisco a few months after Levi died. I was struggling to find a place to share my feelings—a mix of grief, sadness, and gratitude for everything Levi had given me—and there was something truly comforting about being in an environment where other people were sharing so openly about death. I had no plans to speak that night—I had gone just to listen—but after hearing someone share about losing her mom, someone share about losing their childhood friend, and someone share a hilarious poem about losing a stuffed animal that made everyone laugh out loud, I felt like I had to share something about Levi.

After I spoke, I felt as though a huge weight had been lifted off my shoulders. Audience members came up to me and said, "I never met Levi, but now I feel like I got to be with him tonight. Thank you." I felt like other people understood what I was going through; I felt like I wasn't alone. I felt a huge amount of space open up around me. I actually felt ready to go outside and make Levi proud.

In my body, I felt what Ned meant when he described "living in death's face."

Ned is one of the most open, heartfelt, and emotionally vulnerable men I've ever met—I don't think I've ever seen Ned speak for more than twenty seconds without breaking into tears and sharing his love of life. In fact, when I interviewed Ned and You're Going to Die coleader Chelsea Coleman, who is a singer-songwriter and an accountant, Ned started crying on our Zoom call.

When we spoke, Ned and Chelsea were mourning the loss of their friend who had died of cancer the week before. Ned was able to visit her the day before she died, and Chelsea sang a song for her husband and friends during a flower ceremony. It was the first time Chelsea had played live music since the pandemic began, and she told me, "It's good to have a reminder that this work is timeless—we'll always need people to sing for us while our husband and friends are putting flowers on our body."

There's something special about the way friendship is built into the very core of what You're Going to Die represents, both in terms of the community of friends it brings together and how the organization itself is run. Ned and Chelsea decided they only wanted to be working with people they're totally in love with and who they felt better by being with.

Perhaps conversations about death and dying help us see people for who they really are and discover the people we actually want to surround ourselves with and invest in. We're able to see quite clearly what's in front of us. As *New Yorker* writer Hua Hsu puts it, "Stories about love offer models for how you might commit your life to another person. Stories about friendship are usually about how you might commit to life itself."

"Showing up at You're Going to Die signals that you can talk to me about something heavier, something deeper than small talk," Chelsea said, sharing that she got to know her now-husband, Nick, at a You're Going to Die show. "It makes it easier to talk to people. There's so much to connect on after being at a show like that."

"The show is a good space for clearing out the bullshit and immediately dropping in," Ned added. "You're saying, 'Here's where I'm at, really.' That's an invitation for the audience to say, 'More please.'"

PART FOUR

*Stay in Touch*

# BECOME A
# CORRESPONDENCE QUEEN

One of the first people I spoke to when I started writing this book was my friend Paloma Cotton-Herman, who I also call the "Correspondence Queen." Back in the day, when Pal (perfect name for the Correspondence Queen, right?!) and I were roommates in San Francisco, Pal would bust out her correspondence shoebox almost every week. The shoebox was full of letterpress cards, stationery, and stamps. Pal changed schools in middle school and had a consistent friend group from summers, so she was juggling friends from different parts of her life from an early age, and keeping in touch with her people became even more important when she moved across the country at the age of twenty-two, thousands of miles away from family.

I always admired how much time and care Pal put into her correspondence ritual, and it's one of the reasons she is able to maintain close relationships with so many friends from different times in her life. During his toast at Pal's wedding, Pal's father, Jeff, remarked, "Unlike most millennials, Pal actually has real friends not just Facebook friends," and I think that's true.

I asked Pal to share a few tips for staying connected when you feel far away. Here are a few of her recommendations:

**1. Avoid the "out-of-touch" guilt spiral.** Pal knows people who are racked with guilt about not calling that person back or answering a text. Weeks and then months pass, and they feel guilty about dropping the ball, so they never reinitiate communication. Sometimes Pal is in closer touch with a friend due to various circumstances and life stages, and sometimes there are lulls for one reason or another. Pal just accepts that those are chapters and they are likely not malicious; then she is only glad when those chapters open back up.

**2. Invest in correspondence.** Pal jokingly calls purchasing letterpress cards her "most expensive hobby," given that the cards run from four to six dollars and at any given moment, she has about sixty to seventy-five blank ones on hand (who wants to be caught without an occasion-appropriate card?!). That adds up! But through the years, Pal has amassed some favorite card stores, subscribed to their sales, bought in bulk (especially birthday, wedding, and baby cards), and generally felt great about supporting small businesses and artists. That said, Pal will also buy a card here and there for a specific person—she has been known to purchase a spot-on birthday card months and months in advance for someone because it is simply perfect for them. She is incapable of going into a stationery store and not getting at least one card. But everyone in Pal's life benefits (in particular, her wife, who gets to browse their in-home card library for the perfect card).

**3. Write more letters.** Pal enjoys that her favorite hobby, both the purchasing, stamp selecting, and then writing of cards, is anachronistic, and thus people feel special receiving cards among their junk mail and bills. Analog stands out in the age of supreme digital. Pal wonders if she should have lived in the era when everyone was journaling and writing letters, and thus so many more moments would be timestamped. Pal just finished reading *When We Rise* by Cleve Jones, the San Francisco–based AIDS and LGBTQ rights activist. He notes many moments of correspondence and captures exactly how she feels about the lost art: "I miss writing and receiving letters. There was something very satisfying about the writing of them, the dating and location references, the folding and the selection of stationery and stamps. Postal correspondence was something of an art, and the sending and receiving of letters was sort of an exchange of small gifts."

**4. Accept that every friend is different.** Pal thinks understanding and then accepting each friend's individual strengths and challenges, particularly in the communication realm, is tough but important. Some people don't do well with spontaneous phone calls, or texting during the day, or sharing personal information unprompted. Taking these inclinations to mind is a way both to maximize friendships and to show support.

# SEND A VIDEO LOVE LETTER

What happens if a dear friend is thousands of miles away and you want to quickly tell them how much they mean to you? How do you communicate your love in that exact moment? You could send them a text message, or comment on their most recent Facebook post, or slide into their Insta DMs.

But you can also send them a video love letter so they can see your face and feel your energy.

My buddy Andrew Horn's company, Tribute, makes it easy to create short video montage "tributes" for important events in your friends' lives like birthdays, weddings, and graduations; or to send love to someone when they are sick. After Levi passed away, Andrew helped organize a Tribute for Levi's parents so they could watch video messages from people all over the world sharing how much Levi meant to them.

While I was writing this book, my partner organized a beautiful Tribute to celebrate my thirty-seventh birthday. While we were quarantined together, drinking coffee and eating birthday blueberry pancakes on the morning of June 29, 2020, she showed me a thirty-minute Tribute of my closest friends saying really sweet things about me. It felt like they were right there, having breakfast with me. I teared up and wondered how the hell she was able to track down all my homies' emails. It was the most special birthday gift I've ever received, since I couldn't physically be with my friends due to COVID-19.

My sister, Becca, even decided to make a birthday Tribute for her son, Luka, to celebrate his first birthday. Since Luka is only one, the prompt was to share a short piece of advice for eighteen-year-old Luka. My sister is going to wait to share the Tribute until Luka turns eighteen! I can't wait for that moment.

Not long ago, I received a WhatsApp video message from Andrew. He told me, "My favorite kind of people have depth and levity. People that can care about the world, and then, not at all. You're one of those people." When I got this video message from Andrew, it brought a huge smile to my face.

Another great tool for video messages is the app Marco Polo. I first learned about Marco Polo when Levi was on chemo, and we started communicating with the app every day. It was a great way for twenty of Levi's closest friends to stay connected and see Levi every single day, even though we were spread out across the country. Levi's brain was starting to get weaker, so it was a lot easier for him to send a Marco Polo than type a whole sentence. Sometimes he'd just send a five-second video of himself making a funny face to our homies group chat, which was hilarious. The video messages brought us closer together, and every now and then, I still get a Marco Polo from Levi's mom, Bluma, telling me she's thinking of Levi or remembering a funny moment we all shared together.

# PUT FRIENDSHIP ON
# THE CALENDAR

When I was in elementary school, my favorite possession was my weekly planner. Some kids showed off their Super Nintendo games and Reebok Pumps; I liked to bust out my gigantic planner from my Trapper Keeper and show everyone my color-coded calendar system. For each friend I had, I had a different color pen to note when we were hanging out. This explains why—to this day—I consider myself a huge nerd. And why I still love calendars. I still use Moleskine notebooks to keep track of my life, although I have finally evolved to using Google Calendar religiously.

If you want to maintain a friendship in the digital age, you need to put your friend-hangs on the calendar. With everything folks have going on, scheduling phone calls, catch-up walks, and reunion weekends in advance is essential. Putting something on the calendar is the first step to making it a recurring ritual, something that you can plan for and get excited about.

My friend Joanna and her friend Jenny schedule a periodic friend conference call. To make it more official, they have an agenda, just like a business meeting. They talk about their feelings, read their horoscopes, talk about their passion projects, and how they can support each other.

Putting their conference call on their Google Calendar makes it feel official, like it cannot be moved to another date or time.

Every year for the past four years, my buddies and I have gone for a Boys' Hike, our annual five-day backpacking trip in the California wilderness. Our trips have featured a fifty-mile hike along the John Muir Trail in the Sierras, a twenty-five-mile hike to Iva Bell Hot Springs near Mammoth Lakes, and a twenty-mile hike along the Lost Coast Trail in Humboldt County. Even though we all have busy work and personal schedules, we've been able to commit to doing our annual Boys' Hike because we put it on the calendar more than six months out. Once we actually get into the woods, we lose track of time, forget what day it is, and spend hours lying by the stream and soaking in hot springs.

The more you plan ahead, the more fun times you can have with your friends. It's also fun to block some time in your weekly calendar for spontaneity. "Hey, friend, I was just thinking of you. I know it's last minute, but are you free to hang out tonight?!"

# BRING GOOD HABITS HOME

One of the most formative experiences in my life was studying abroad. I spent a semester during the spring of my junior year of college studying Latin American cinema and living in Havana, Cuba. I wanted to expose myself to a completely different culture. I learned that you can't just follow what popular opinion would have you believe; you have to go see a place for yourself.

I also learned just how powerful travel can be to make new friendships. In Havana, I fell deeply in love for the first time in my life. I also met friends who I've stayed in touch with ever since. My two closest buddies from that trip (we call ourselves "Los Tres") have stayed in touch for almost twenty years. Whenever we get together, we still reminisce about walking the streets of Havana among the cars from the 1950s, dancing salsa, drinking too much rum, going to Santería ceremonies, and taking a train across the island.

I recently spoke with my friend Hayli, who traveled away from her home in San Diego for nearly four years. Her leaving was born of not having a community, feeling like she had not found her people, and wondering why she had so many shallow friendships. Interestingly enough, when Hayli left, she went to a small remote village on the island of Sumatra, in Indonesia, where English was hardly spoken.

Because of the linguistic barriers, Hayli didn't have a conversation for nearly six months, but she recalls still being able to connect with the people she met. "Art was the language I spoke," she recalls. "I had profound interactions, usually around art or music or food, and I remember them as if they were conversations. What I learned to appreciate was our interconnectedness and our shared humanity, which is a lot more important than talking."

The village she first spent time in had experienced a devastating flood in 2003, taking the lives of hundreds of people. She learned that the way the community was healing and rebuilding was what mattered most. "They were talking about shared trauma," Hayli remembers. "They were rallying around each other, singing songs, music was playing out of every home. There was a real culture of healing, and everyone was contributing to this community."

Hayli continued her travels to Cambodia, Vietnam, and Malaysia, but she has been back to Sumatra three times now, and she describes people she met there as family. She built really profound relationships that expand past space and time. "If you go in from a place of depth, if that's where you begin," Hayli told me, "then you can totally not see someone for three years and still have the depth of the moment of the first time you met them."

Traveling helped Hayli learn how to appreciate people, how to be open and receptive to people different than her. "Before I left, I wasn't accepting people for who they were, I wasn't seeing them in their totality as a human being, with their traumas, their successes, all the things that had been a part of leading them to this moment," she recalls.

When we spoke, Hayli was back home in San Diego, happy and feeling like she had finally found her people and her community. After spending so much time living in cultures where access to technology is limited or unavailable, Hayli has made cultivating presence a practice she lives by. When she meets new people, she spends time just being with them, sometimes not even talking. Hayli told me that choosing not to have a SIM card for her travels was one of the best things she ever did, because she could only interact with what was happening right in front of her.

"In Europe, when you go out for a three-hour dinner, no one is on their phone," Hayli said. "People are present with their company." Now when she meets up with friends or meets someone new, Hayli avoids looking at her phone and tries to just be with the person she's interacting with, as if she were still in Sumatra. She frequently sends postcards to let people know she is thinking of them. If a friend tells her they are going through a rough time, she sends them a book that could help (or help cheer them up).

There's a difference between exploring a foreign country (or exploring your own neighborhood) with your head buried in Google Maps, Instagram, and a list of the "coolest places to see," and simply looking up and noticing what seems interesting and talking to the people you come across on your journey. I'm so grateful that I didn't own a cell phone back when I studied abroad in Cuba in 2003. I'm sure that experience would not have been as powerful. "Travel showed me the world is not on a two-by-two square on your social media feed," says Hayli. "It's all around you. And if you're not engaging with all these things around you, you're missing the whole world that's right there."

# KEEP A FRIEND
# TREASURE BOX

Remember Kodak Fun Savers? The disposable yellow cameras you used to get at CVS for fifteen dollars? You could bring them to school or camp or on a trip somewhere, take a bunch of pictures, and then be surprised when you finally got your film developed a month later. I loved the anticipation of waiting at CVS, not knowing exactly what was going to come out of the photo machine. It's almost as if you got to relive your adventure all over again, looking through the photos, since they were relics of a past experience. Plus, when you had all your pictures printed, you could cut them up into photo album scrapbooks. My sister would write down descriptions and quotes next to each photo. On a recent trip to our parents' house, she and I looked through her old photo books from summer camp and we spent hours cracking up.

In the era of minimalism and tidying up, it's common to throw things like printed photos from CVS in the garbage. What most people are left with is a massive iPhoto album of thousands of photos (that you never really go back and look at) or a memory log limited to their Instagram feed. But what about life before your iPhone? What about life before Instagram?

*Hold on to the
handwritten notes,
the ticket stubs,
the photos,
the little tokens
of friendship that
make you remember
everything.*

I'm in favor of holding on to objects that bring me joy. I don't want all of my memories to be digitized. To this end, I keep a few shoeboxes full of old photos in my closet. Once a year, usually between Christmas and New Year's, I have a ritual where I sift through my old photos while listening to the Postal Service album "Give Up." It makes me nostalgic for the early-aughts every single time. I also sift through my Friend Treasure Box. It's an old cigar box full of mementos that remind me of people, places, and things I love. Here are a few things in my Friend Treasure Box:

A photo of dinner with my grandmother, my parents, and my best friend, Dre, the night before college graduation in 2005 (Dre and I stayed up all night and nearly missed our graduation ceremony. Dre lost his keys and had to climb headfirst into our first-floor window to get his cap and gown in front of his entire family. We were thirty seconds away from missing the processional.)

A ticket stub from Game 5 of the American League Championship Series at Fenway Park, October 18, 2004. (Perhaps the best game in baseball history, the Red Sox beat the Yankees in fourteen innings—the game lasted five hours and forty-nine minutes. Dre nearly fell off the Green Monster because he couldn't take the drama. We bumped into my childhood buddy Dan and his dad, Eddie, after the game, and I jumped with so much joy into Eddie's arms that he nearly toppled over.)

A ticket stub to the Obama for America Staff Ball on January 22, 2009 (Celebrating Barack Obama's victory in Washington, DC, with my fellow campaign staffers. Arcade Fire *and* Jay-Z played a private show for us that night, and we were so hopeful for the future.)

I also keep postcards and handwritten notes in my Friendship Treasure Box. Whenever I visit my parents' house, my mom sneaks a postcard into my bag before I leave. Even though she's done it dozens of times since I was a little kid, it still feels like a surprise every single time, and I love reading these notes when I get on the airplane. I've even caught my mom slipping the card in my bag, but it doesn't matter. I still get excited to read my mom's postcards. My favorite postcard ever was one of a guy holding up a sign for the Fung Wah Bus—a bus that I took dozens of times in my twenties to go from Boston to New York City for only fifteen dollars.

We throw enough stuff away. Hold on to the handwritten notes, the ticket stubs, the photos, the little tokens of friendship that make you remember everything.

# PICK UP THE PHONE AND CALL

How often have you heard someone say, "I am not good at staying in touch." In the digital age, this is a cop-out, as meaningless as saying "I'm really busy these days." Being busy isn't an excuse for not staying in touch with the people you care about most.

Call me *old school*, but my favorite method of catch-up with friends who don't live near me is to pick up the phone and call. It's great to schedule calls ahead of time, but sometimes I love to just pick up the phone and call someone when I want to talk with them. If they are busy or don't pick up, I leave a voicemail, and they call me back. These calls generally last about an hour—I try to make at least two per week—and they are the highlight of my week. I like the phone call because I have trouble sitting still. While I'm catching up with a buddy, I can take a walk outside and get some exercise, clean my room, wait in line at Trader Joe's, or even cook dinner.

If you don't think you have two or three hours a week to call someone you love, I'd challenge you to track how much time you spend weekly on social media, checking email, reading the news, or watching Netflix. You have *plenty* of time. In the words of Dan Rather, "That person you keep thinking, 'I should call them.' You should. Do it. Pass it on."

Maybe you're not a fan of the phone call—that's okay—the important thing is that you check in with your besties. Maybe it's weekly, maybe it's monthly, maybe it's every two or three months. Embrace the check-in. As my friend Paloma, the Correspondence Queen, says, "Find your medium! Maybe it is not the phone or epic written letters, but a pithy text every so often. Or sending an article that reminds you of a certain person. Or a group email to your loved ones every so often. Having friends from all eras in life, of all lengths of time—even just a few—is proven to boost happiness. And as we continue to enter new life stages and changes, these check-ins, however consistent or inconsistent, have proven critical for me."

Instead of the phone call, my friend Hana Nobel sends a monthly "holiday postcard" to her friends—even where there isn't a holiday to celebrate. She's been sending holiday cards just of herself since college, and this year she jokingly invited people to receive one every month. To her surprise, more than seventy people asked to receive one. Every month she sends out a picture of herself, sometimes themed with a seasonal message or whatever she feels like writing. "People are happy to get mail that's not bills," says Hana.

Another friend of mine, Adam Greenberg, created a Facebook event event for his twenty-sixth birthday and invited people to write him a snail-mailed letter, as short or as long as they wanted, about something from their time together, and he promised to respond to everyone. He received more than one hundred letters and responded to all of them. Now nearly a decade later, he told me he still remembers this as an excellent gift to himself and a nice way to reconnect with friends.

# LISTEN TO A FULL ALBUM

How do you make friends? You can find people with similar interests, but you can also find people you just want to chill with. My friend Sara Weinberg once told me that her measurement of friendship is "How easy is it to sit on the couch and do nothing with somebody?" Unstructured free time is something a lot of us aren't very good at these days. We're so distracted with our phones, watching videos online, or consuming social media that sometimes we forget how to be still and kick it with someone.

In college, I spent most of my unstructured free time listening to music with my buddies. That was back in the early 2000s, when everyone had two or three Case Logic CD cases filled with all their music, and my measure of friendship compatibility was checking out someone's CD collection.

I remember going to a party at 84 High Street, an off-campus house at Wesleyan University, and going upstairs to chill in this kid Kevin's room. The walls of his room were painted turquoise and purple, there were tamari-roasted almonds and ginger chews sitting on the coffee table, and the Flaming Lips album *Yoshimi Battles the Pink Robots* was playing on the stereo. I was *feeling* this kid's room. We smoked a joint, and I checked out Kevin's CD collection. I flipped through the pages of

Kevin's Case Logic CD case and noticed some of my favorites: *Homogenic* by Björk, *KID A* by Radiohead, *The Moon & Antarctica* by Modest Mouse, *Deadringer* by RJD2, *Michigan* by Sufjan Stevens, and *Train of Thought* by Talib Kweli and Hi-Tek.

I think we listened to all of *KID A* and *Amnesiac* that day. I was like, "Yo, Kevin, pass the tamari-roasted almonds. Also, can we be friends?"

Nearly twenty years later, Kevin and I have traveled together across Argentina, we've hiked numerous mountains, we've been there for each other during breakups with girlfriends, and we've supported each other through moves from the East Coast to the West Coast to the East Coast and back to the West Coast again. If someone has good taste in music—and heady snacks—if you can sit on the couch and chill with them while you listen to an entire Radiohead album (or two Radiohead albums)—hold on to them at all costs.

# KEEP FRIENDSHIP IN YOUR FAMILY MANIFESTO

There aren't a lot of blueprints out there for how to maintain your friendships once you have a partner and children. Nearly every parent I spoke to told me they wished they had more time to spend with their friends.

According to my friends Ted and Franziska Gonder, the secret to making life more fulfilling as a new-ish, young-ish parent is being incredibly dedicated to their three children and making the right decisions as a family unit. Ted and Franzi are both ambitious entrepreneurs who were deeply focused on building their own start-ups and businesses when they met in their mid-twenties. They made a decision early on in their relationship to move closer to Franzi's family in the suburbs of Düsseldorf, Germany, not because that's what would be best for either of them as individual entrepreneurs, or because they thought the coolest people lived in the suburbs of Düsseldorf, but because that's what was going to work best for them as a couple and as a family.

Ted and Franzi wanted to build a relationship where they were involved in different aspects of each other's lives, where they were partners in building a life together, not just partners who spent time together on the weekends. They made it a goal to maximize the amount of time they spent together as a family unit and maximize the amount they understood each other as a couple.

This intention dated back to the early months of their relationship, before Ted and Franzi even started dating, when they were just getting to know each other long distance. They created a shared Google doc where they each answered five questions every week:

*How are you?*
*What's a dream you have for us to do together?*
*What's one thing that puzzles you about me?*
*What's one thing you'd like to see me change?*
*What's one thing you appreciated about me last week?*

Sharing these answers brought Ted and Franzi closer together and helped them think about what kind of life they wanted to design together. They decided to make a family manifesto, full of things they want to live and feel every day. "Love is a start-up. It's a little company you're building, with all the highs and lows, with a mission and a vision," Franzi told me.

I love the idea of creating a family manifesto, and it occurs to me that so few families actually take the time to reflect on how they want to be and live and feel together. Or how they want to exist as lovers, parents, friends, professionals, and community members. By having a clear vision and making decisions as an entrepreneurial family unit of five individuals, Ted and Franzi have been able to get through challenging times and weather the loneliness that comes from living in a country thousands of miles away from some of their closest friends. While they miss their best friends immensely, they don't feel alone; they feel very socially enriched. "I'm married to my best friend, and my kids are super fun," Ted said. "You always have someone to talk to when you're married to your best friend."

Rather than individual godparents, Ted and Franzi have a "god-board" of six people for all three of their kids (Maxi, who is five years old; Benji, two; and Atlas, one). This provides community-based answers to important family decisions and also brings the most important people into their family's life forever. I used to think of assigning godparents as a rather old-fashioned, religious practice that made me think of the Catholic Church and Marlon Brando. But many families are reclaiming the tradition as a way to ensure your closest friends remain in your life after you have children. When my best friend, Dre, and his partner, Manuela, asked me to be their son Diego's godfather, it felt like a true honor. Diego is only three years old, but I've seen him grow up because I visit him whenever I'm in Boston. Over time, Diego and I are developing a deep friendship, just like the one I have with his dad.

Ted and Franzi have individual email newsletters related to their personal careers, but they also have a joint family newsletter that goes to fifty friends once or twice a year. Their family newsletter includes a few stories and family photos and major family updates. It's an informal way to stay in touch with everyone back home in the United States, tell their friends they love them, and ask if there are any major updates in their lives. Once their kids are older, and when Ted and Franzi need less support from their parents, they would like to move back to the United States. Knowing them, I'm sure they'll make a thoughtful decision based on what's best for their very best friends: their family.

# BUILD A HEALTHIER RELATIONSHIP WITH SOCIAL MEDIA

---

One of the funny things about being a counselor thirteen different times at Camp Grounded, a tech-free summer camp, was learning that the majority of campers heard about camp from a friend sharing their experience on Facebook. Isn't that ironic? People are coming to a transformational experience that's a *digital detox*, but they never would have heard about it if they weren't using their devices and social media. Such is the delicate balance of the world we live in.

In a popular video about the loneliness epidemic, journalist Johann Hari cites the work of John Cacioppo, one of the world's leading scholars on loneliness, who believed that social media could in fact bring people closer together *if* it were being used as a waystation for people to actually meet in person. That is to say, if people are using apps and websites to meet like-minded people or discover transformational experiences like Camp Grounded, and then they actually go offline to meet up with these people in real life, they can bring us closer together. But if you're only using the apps to connect online and you're never going offscreen—if tech is the final destination and not the place where you find directions—then these tools will lead to increased isolation and its negative side effects.

My intention is to get you to spend as little time as possible on social media, but because I'm realistic about the fact that most people—including me—are going to keep using these apps, here are a few ways I recommend making your time spent on social media a little more effective:

**Real talk beats bragging.** Celebrating major life accomplishments is awesome, but we all know that life is not a constant highlight reel. When I was experiencing increased loneliness, it felt reassuring to share my real feelings with others. I realized I wasn't alone and that a lot of people were struggling with the same things—even people who, from the looks of social media, were as happy as could be. Be open and honest and real with your feelings. Share lows and struggles and challenges, especially if you want to make a change in your life.

**Heavy moments are best unpacked with professionals.** Your Facebook friends, although well-intentioned, might not be the right people to consult when it comes to dealing with really hard things. Social media is a pretty awful place to be spending time when you're unwell. Consider spending less time online and more time talking to a therapist, mental health professional, family member, or someone you trust when confronting something traumatic or sensitive.

**Open, don't close, dialogue.** Netflix's documentary *The Social Dilemma* captures the extent to which social media has contributed to society's increased polarization and extremism. Social media is not an easy place to respectfully disagree. Nuance, tact, and grace don't often find a welcome home on a Facebook comment thread. A 2017 study by the Pew Research Center showed that posts exhibiting "indignant disagreement" received nearly twice as much engagement as other types of content on Facebook. Another study by William J. Brady and his colleagues at NYU found that each moral or emotional word in a tweet increased its virality by 20 percent. If you engage in political or difficult conversations on social media, whenever possible, seek ways to open rather than close dialogue. Call in rather than call out. Avoid shaming, hold back judgment, and try to assume the best intentions, even if someone posts something you vehemently disagree with. If you're interested in going deeper, ask someone if they're available to discuss their feelings offline, on a phone call, or in person. Or, simply state, "Thanks for sharing your thoughts. I'd love to discuss this another time with you offline."

**Promote your friends.** Take a break from your highlight reel to celebrate a friend. Maybe your friend just wrote a book, got a new job, or is raising money for an important cause. I recently made an intention to make a "friend in need" post at least once a month. This means if I have a friend looking for a new job or one looking for a publisher for their book, I will make a Facebook post on their behalf. Using my network to lift up someone I love seems like as good a use of social media as any.

**Offer compliments.** You don't even need a reason to celebrate your friends. I recently saw a Facebook post by my buddy Nick Baker, which read, "People of the Earth, I present to you the magnificent Will! Today, like a bolt of lightning to the heart, I was struck with electric pulses of gratitude for this dear friend. It isn't his birthday. He's not sick. He didn't die. This isn't a fund-raiser. This is simply a for-no-good-reason 'love up' of a man who gives so much goodness to the world . . . . Love him up in the comments to fill in all the parts I missed if the spirit moves you!" Nick's post received seventy comments, and I'm sure it made Will's day and inspired a few others to do the same for their friends.

Earlier I mentioned my friend Bailey Robinson, who will occasionally post on Facebook, "Comment on this post if you need some words of affirmation." She then gives someone love and positive reflections right then and there on the comment thread. If someone keeps popping up on the thread, Bailey will reach out to them and check in, sharing, "I'm here to articulate the magic you didn't even know you were making," a great example of using tech to foster emotional connection.

# MAKE VIRTUAL CONNECTION A REALITY

In the early days of the pandemic, like many people, I experienced intense Zoom fatigue. I thought to myself, *I miss live events! I'm already tired of Zoom and it's only week one of shelter-in-place. I don't want to go to your Zoom happy hour, I want to hang out with you in real life. I want to see you and be able to look into your eyes and hug you!* As I started settling into the new normal, I realized that Zoom life was not going away anytime soon and that—while surely less exciting than in-person connection—virtual connection is very possible to achieve, but it requires reimagining and redesigning how we gather folks online.

"At most in-person events, attendees connect at a lunch break, while waiting in line for the restroom, or at a casual happy hour," writes connection expert Jenny Sauer-Klein. "We assume these moments of serendipity will be enough to check off the boxes for 'networking' and 'building community.' However, in a virtual context, there is no opportunity for connection by accident—we must design for connection on purpose."

Jenny recommends three design principles for creating connection virtually: **connect early, connect often,** and **gradually invite deeper levels of vulnerability**. For connecting early, instead of hosting a webinar where the audience is muted and passively watching a slide show presentation, the host would instead invite audience members to participate immediately. For example, when I hosted my Author Support Group on Zoom, I would play music as attendees arrived and welcome folks by name as they entered the Zoom. I'd then invite folks to share a "win" from their week in the chat window. The first activity would be in a breakout room, where attendees could share in pairs what progress they had made writing their book. Then, I'd break participants into another breakout room so they could share one-on-one with someone else. Within the first ten minutes of the virtual event, I made it clear that active participation would be required of the attendees. This wasn't a webinar where you just sat back and watched while you ate popcorn on the couch.

In the course of our ninety-minute sessions on Zoom, there were multiple breakout rooms and Q&A sessions, creating opportunities for what Jenny refers to as connecting often. You can't just do an icebreaker and then expect people to be engaged for an hour or two. People want as much opportunity to talk to each other as possible. In the feedback forms for Author Support Group, nearly everyone mentioned that what they found most useful was the community, the chance to build relationships with other authors.

In other words, people are looking for online connection much more than they are looking for online content. There are fifty thousand blog posts out there about how to build an online course, but few people actually want more slide decks. They want a place to open up and talk to other people. Of course, you don't want to ask people to share their deepest fear within five minutes of arriving to a Zoom meeting; you have to gradually invite deeper levels of vulnerability and establish trust first, just as you would in person. One way to do this is to add rituals to virtual meetings, such as an opening dance party, a minute of silent reflection or breathwork, or an artifact share where everyone takes turns sharing about an object of personal relevance from wherever they're calling.

During the pandemic, my friend Kat Vellos reminded me that there's more than one way to be connected from afar. Despite the fact that everyone and their grandmother was spending eight hours a day on

Zoom, it doesn't mean that's the best way to connect virtually. Kat is a proponent of screenless connecting, even remotely. Kat began hosting a Connection Club—"a nerdy, loving club that's a mix between study hall, art club, and accountability buddies"—a supportive and creative place to nurture your bonds and feel closer to your friends. One of the weekly rituals during Connection Club was a letter-writing ritual. Participants would join the call and write letters together from afar, off camera, and Kat would DJ the call so everyone was listening to the same music. After writing letters, folks could come on camera and stay on the call if they wanted to chat with other Connection Club members.

Kat's friend Lucy Bellwood started an experimental voicemail box during quarantine called the Right Number ("a place to speak and be heard"), where she posted a phone number and a prompt to respond to via a voicemail message. Prompts like "What do you wish you could say to someone right now?" rotated every two weeks, and all messages were confidential, kind of like an open confessional box, for which only Lucy could hear the final messages.

As the pandemic wore on, I became more hopeful about the potential for virtual platforms to bring us closer together. While it's certainly not easy, if we become more intentional and, as Jenny reminds us, *design for connection on purpose*, we can make virtual connection a reality, not just a tired Silicon Valley sales pitch.

# A Few Apps That Help You Connect with Friends

While it's my intention to help you spend *less* time looking at your phone, if you're struggling to meet new people, here are a few apps and websites that help you actually meet people and spend more time with like-minded humans. Friendly reminder to exercise caution when meeting new people online: do your due diligence and prioritize your safety.

**Meetup:** A service used to organize online groups that host in-person events for people with similar interests.

**Eventbrite:** An event management and ticketing website that allows you to see events and experiences happening near you.

**Nextdoor:** A private social network for your neighborhood community.

**Marco Polo:** A video communication app that helps you feel close, even when life gets busy.

**Houseparty:** A social networking app that allows up to eight people to video chat at once in a "room."

**Clubhouse:** Social platform with voice-only discussion rooms.

**Cuppa:** Have 1:1 virtual coffees with curious minds from Twitter.

**Lunchclub:** Curated 1:1 professional connections based on your background, goals, and interests.

**Meet My Dog:** Enables dog owners to discover, connect, and share with other dog owners in their community.

**Bumble BFF:** The friendship mode of the Bumble dating app.

**Hey! VINA:** Tinder for (girl) friends. Swipe right to meet new friends and join communities of people like you.

**Donut:** A Slack app that helps connect teams serendipitously for virtual coffee, peer learning, and more.

**Nearify:** Discover events near you like live music, comedy, concerts, festivals, theater, and more.

**ATLETO:** Connects you with like-minded athletes based on location, skill level, frequency, and mode to provide the best sports experience possible.

**Peanut:** Shows you like-minded mothers near you and makes it easier to meet.

**Friender:** Connects people with common interests.

**We3:** Find the most awesome people nearby; meet new friends in groups of three.

**MeetMe:** Meet, chat, and have fun with new people.

**Squad:** An invite-only community for millennials and Gen-Zers looking to move beyond the screen and build real-life connections.

**Hylo:** Community management, messaging, and collaboration all in one place.

**Dex:** A personal Customer Relationship Management (CRM) app that helps you build stronger relationships.

**Fabriq:** Prioritize and track your most important relationships: get reminders to reach out consistently.

**Bloom:** Online experiences exclusively for people over the age of fifty to connect.

**Stitch:** Community and companionship for anyone over fifty.

**REALU:** Find real people in real time; meet interesting people near you; do something with them in the real world.

**Tribute:** Makes it easy to create a collaborative video montage that you can give as a gift on any important occasion.

**Evlyn:** A mobile application for storing messages for loved ones and distributing them when you pass away.

**Dial Up:** A voice-chat app that connects you serendipitously to the people you want to stay in touch with.

**Walkie:** A community where you say what you want to talk about and get to have a phone call with an interested person right away.

**Listenly:** Schedule a listening session with an experienced, trained listener.

**Mon Ami:** Volunteer management technology to make it easier to coordinate volunteer efforts and build connections across generations in a time of need.

**Goodnight Zoom:** Remote storytelling with an isolated senior.

**Papa:** Pairs older adults and families with Papa Pals for companionship and assistance with everyday tasks.

**Meals Together:** Creating companionship through intergenerational dinner parties over video calls.

# USE TECHNOLOGY TO HEAL

Technology certainly has contributed to our loneliness epidemic, but the internet can be a powerful tool to facilitate human connection and friendship, especially for those without anyone else to turn to. My friend Liz Travis Allen was bitten by a tick in 2003, and she went from being a two-sport Division 1 athlete to being bed-bound and experiencing symptoms like chronic debilitating pain, intense fatigue, headaches, muscle aches, and shortness of breath. For the last seventeen years, she's been fighting to regain her health in a health care system that doesn't quite understand how to cure her immune system. Like thousands of others with post-treatment Lyme disease (she has also been diagnosed with chronic fatigue syndrome), Liz has had to figure out on her own what treatments work and what medications she needs to take.

Liz told me that it was impossible for her "able-bodied friends" to understand her disability. She struggled and felt isolated and alone, all while trying to make sense of her chronic pain. It was only when she met other people like her on the internet that she felt a sense of emotional resonance and belonging. She saw that there was a hashtag for Lyme disease on Instagram and that people all over the world were sharing their experiences with the disease. She created a second Instagram account that was her "sick account," and she found a whole community of people who were chronically sick, couldn't leave home, and were sharing openly about their experiences being sick, what treatments they were trying, what medications were working and not working, and how the world was treating others with disabilities. In short, she realized that she wasn't alone.

Liz forged deep friendships with some of the people she was following on Instagram. She joined online communities like Tired Girl Society (a space for women to meet online and find solace from the isolation of living with illness) and More Than Lyme (which raises awareness of Lyme disease through adventure, events, and storytelling), and used group chat threads and her new friendships to find all of her treatment programs, her team of doctors, and an experimental combination of medications that actually made her feel better.

"Joining these communities gave me my health back," Liz told me. "They were absolutely critical for my well-being as a human." Liz is no longer bed-bound and now is able to hold down a job and socialize with her peers. She went from a critical condition to managing a condition with a fairly regular life through the advice given to her on the internet.

During quarantine, Liz shared her advice as someone who had been self-isolating for seventeen years because of her disease. She wanted to make sure her "healthy friends" knew that the anger, grief, restlessness, boredom, and anxiety would come and go.

"Eventually, the isolation ends," she said. "I feel better, and when I venture outside, the whole world feels reborn. The flowers glow, and the sunshine looks like spun white gold. Small talk is novel, people in the park a delight, every step outside screams of freedom. Gratitude oozes out my pores. I marinate in bliss."

Liz's story reminds us that well-being looks different for everyone, that there's always someone out there who might know what you're going through, and that technology sometimes has the power to heal.

# PART FIVE

# *Embrace Ritual*

# REPLACE SCROLLING
# WITH GRATITUDE

Recent studies have shown that a regular practice of expressing gratitude changes the structure of the brain, makes us healthier and happier,
and can be associated with better sleep and lower levels of anxiety and
depression. Meanwhile, increased social media use has been tied to feelings of isolation and loneliness, especially among young people.

For the first year I was on Instagram, I actually thought that
#latergram meant that you were taking a break from Instagram, as in
you post such a dope photo that you're like "Peace out Instagram. I'm
going to hang out with my friends, byeeeeeeee!"

Unfortunately, that's not what #latergram means. All too often I
feel pressure from some universal higher power to constantly be sharing my whereabouts, opinions, and accomplishments. I've experienced
intense periods of scrolling aimlessly, jealous of the highlight reels of
my friends, comparing myself to their beautiful lives, wishing I were
traveling wherever they were, dating someone like the person they
were dating, and generally just feeling sad and sorry for myself. There
are days when I feel like I can't relax until I've posted something. It's
ridiculous, yet the pressure is very real. Instagram Stories makes this
even worse; some of my thirty-something-year-old friends share their

highlights almost *constantly*—and these are grown-ass adults who came of age without cell phones, getting dysentery playing *Oregon Trail*. Think about how bad it must be for kids and teenagers who have never known a world without smartphones!

Whenever I start to feel this way, I take a one-week Social Media Sabbatical. Instead of using social media, I practice gratitude for a week. Every evening before bed, I think of two people in my life I care about, and the next day, I call them completely out of the blue to let them know why I am grateful for them. Sometimes they pick up the phone and we get to have a completely spontaneous catch-up phone call. Sometimes they don't pick up (because they might be distracted, watching Instagram Stories)—all good. I leave a voicemail. By the end of the week, I've gotten to tell fourteen people how much they mean to me. If you're worried you don't have time to call fourteen people this week, add up how much time you spent scrolling on social media. I guarantee you have enough time and that time is better spent expressing gratitude than looking at #latergram pics.

# CREATE A UNIQUE ROUTINE

When I lived in Brooklyn after college, I had lunch with my grandmother every Friday. I took the F train to meet Gran at her apartment on East Tenth Street, by Washington Square Park in Manhattan, and we'd walk to a nearby restaurant on the corner of Tenth Street and Broadway called Silver Spurs. I loved our walks, mostly because Gran was the slowest walker I've ever met. Silver Spurs was only two blocks away, but it took us about half an hour to get there. We'd say hi to Gran's neighbor, buy a perfectly ripe peach at the fruit stand, and stop at the ATM so I could help Gran take out cash for the week.

Gran would hold my arm and ask me questions about how work was going and if I was dating anyone. I so badly wanted to tell her, "Gran, I met her! I met my person! I'm in love!"—I think she probably would have done a backflip. When we got to Silver Spurs, we'd sit in the same exact booth, with the same server (Pablo) every single time. Gran ordered the exact same meal every week: a bacon cheeseburger with French fries and coffee, and I ordered a bagel with lox and cream cheese and a coffee, at which point Gran would ask if I wanted an orange juice, and I'd say "no," and Gran would say, "Just get the orange juice!" and I'd say, "Okay, and a large orange juice, please." If our booth wasn't available, we'd wait for it. One Friday, Pablo wasn't working and Gran decided she wasn't hungry and we left.

Even though my grandmother passed away nine years ago, and even though Silver Spurs closed a year after that, every time I'm in New York City, I try to walk by that street corner because it makes me smile. I remember how Gran always said that when she died, she wanted a third of her ashes scattered inside a Hershey's chocolate bar, a third scattered inside Bloomingdale's, and a third scattered at the checkout counter at Gristedes supermarket by her apartment.

Just as I did with Gran, I try to create a unique routine and ritual with each of my friends. It's kind of like in *Seinfeld*: Jerry, George, Elaine, and Kramer always have coffee in the same booth at Monk's Café.

Routine builds comfort, and comfort allows friendship to blossom. I have boys' yoga night with Milo and Kevin; coffee and Wilco with Gabe; dumpling time with Kelsey; vegan ramen with Satya; fresh-caught sushi with Alex, Matt, and Saya; margaritas and mole with Bizzle in Philly; annual Korean BBQ with Bricky, Bubbles, and Blue Bear in LA; burgers with Dre in Cambridge; Code Names with Brady; and Sibling Sunday with my sister.

Clearly, most of my routines are centered around food, but the point is, having a routine where you do the same thing with someone every time you see them can create a powerful home for any relationship.

*Routine builds comfort,
and comfort allows
friendship to blossom.*

# SWIM IN A CREATIVE CONTAINER

One of the most beautiful parts of Camp Grounded was that Levi brought so many creative people together and gave them permission to share their creative gifts, whether those gifts were drawing, songwriting, crocheting, stilt-walking, spoken word, meditating, laughter yoga, pickling, solar carving, choir, stand-up comedy, superfood truffle-making, or cuddle therapy. Camp often felt like being in a swimming pool of creativity; in every direction you looked, from campers practicing improv together to performing the song they just wrote together, people were always making and sharing their unique, eclectic art.

There's something rare and powerful about providing a space for friends to get messy and make magic together. It takes away this expectation that our creativity has to be for money, fame, or follows. It affirms that creating things can be about playing with friends and not figuring out how to profit from them. In one of my favorite TED Talks, actor Joseph Gordon-Levitt says, "If your creativity is driven by a desire to get attention, you're never going to be creatively fulfilled."

One of my fellow camp counselors was Alexis (aka Inspector Bucket), who went to Jewish youth group and has been involved with theater productions since she was young. During the talent show at camp, Alexis and her best friend, Panda, would do an act where they played an older, bickering, Jewish couple—Muriel and Morty—who had been together forever. The act would always bring everyone to laughter, especially since Muriel and Morty would sometimes reappear onstage throughout the show (for example, to rap Shaggy's "It Wasn't Me"). Alexis told me that playing older characters and imagining an older friendship not only brought Muriel and Morty together but made the real-life Alexis and Panda feel like they had a lifetime of knowing each other.

In other words, theater was a vehicle for deepening their friendship. This is something I hear again and again: so many people become friends in a moment or space of artistic expression and creative freedom.

"In performance, I get the permission to experience other people's imaginary stories; the permission to do that in a contained setting creates a level of pleasure and trust that's unique," Alexis explained to me. "From my experiences with camp and theatrical productions, I think there is something very powerful, transcendent, and lasting about building a temporary container where everyone inside the container needs to trust each other fairly quickly in order to make it happen. It creates an intimacy and playfulness that extend beyond the short experience."

If you've ever worked on a theater or film production, helped produce an event, or participated in a creative endeavor, you likely can resonate with the feeling of becoming very close to your peers very quickly. One day you're playing an icebreaker to get to know each other. The next, you're going out for coffee. And a few days later, you're sleeping over at each other's apartments and scheming about writing a screenplay together. Simple acts of creativity fuel more creativity. In Alexis's words, "Creative friendships make me feel like anything is possible both between us and about what we're making."

During COVID-19, Alexis began hosting a weekly Virtual Salon on Zoom to support creative works in progress. She never knows exactly who's going to show up. There is both a core group of people who have become close as well as new people who drop in every week to listen and collaborate on each other's work. The formula is very simple. There's a container with safety and boundaries. Everyone is welcome to share and receive feedback on a creative project they are dreaming up or working on. If no one wants to share, that's okay, too; they just have a conversation about what they're feeling in the moment, which Alexis told me is sometimes just as valuable as talking about their actual projects. The lesson is that it's important to create a canvas for people to try out, test out, and play with their creativity.

Another actor, Ethan Hawke, put it beautifully when he said, "[Creativity] is vital. It's the way we heal each other. In singing our song, in telling our story, in inviting you to say, 'Hey, listen to me, and I'll listen to you,' we're starting a dialogue. And when you do that, this healing happens, and we come out of our corners, and we start to witness each other's common humanity. We start to assert it. And when we do that, really good things happen."

Whenever someone tells me they are struggling to make new friends, I ask them, "When's the last time you performed or sang or built or designed or imagined something with a group of people?" Finding a swimming pool for your creativity—and a place to support others' creativity—will open up a world of possibility.

# HOST A FRIENDS' SHOWCASE

Earlier I mentioned my friends Amber and Farhad's wedding in Marrakech, Morocco. Much more than a celebration of their love for each other, their wedding was a celebration of their love of their community, or "soul fam" as they called us. The wedding weekend was all about creating opportunities for their friends from different parts of life to connect authentically and intentionally. Amber designed a newspaper with headshots of all the guests, with each of our love languages and how we would describe our essence in one word. She also reached out to several friends and asked them to contribute to the wedding beyond the typical ask of giving a toast. One friend was deemed the "Minister of Vibes" and was in charge of always making sure the music was on point. Another friend who's a professional singer emceed a talent show. Two other friends who are experienced coaches facilitated the wedding ceremony.

If you're hosting a gathering, allow your friends to share their unique gifts. Not only will they feel seen and included, but the rest of your community will be inspired to contribute more fully as well. If you think some of your guests don't have anything to offer, think again. Every person in your life brings a unique passion or hobby or gift to the table. For example, at my friend Jenny Klein's wedding, she asked her friend, who is an organic cannabis grower in California, to roll a few joints for the dance party. Her friend ended up rolling one hundred (yes, one hundred!) homegrown joints and served them on a tray like a cocktail waiter would. Rather than a few people trying to hide in the corner while getting high, this contribution became a group ritual that everyone— even the aunts and uncles—could participate in. When's the last time you were served an organic, hand-rolled joint on a platter?! Jenny told me it's still the thing people remember most from the wedding.

You don't have to wait for your wedding as an excuse. In the next month, I invite you to host a friends' showcase in your home or at an event space (or virtually on Zoom). Pick ten of your favorite creative people, and ask them to sing a song, recite a poem, do stand-up comedy, share a story, lead a meditation, or play a game. Invite a bunch of people to experience the power of your friends' creativity. By bringing folks together, you might even inspire your friends—and strangers—to make magic with each other and start working together.

# DON'T GO OUT FOR DRINKS

When I was in my early twenties, I lived in a one-bedroom railroad apartment in Brooklyn with my two best friends from college and our cat, Rooibos. Jesse (aka "the Bizzle") lived in the one actual bedroom, Dre lived in a closet, and my room was the hallway between Bizzle's room and the living room. It was tight, but we didn't care. It was our first adult apartment, and we were just happy to be living somewhere other than our parents' houses.

I remember drinking heavily in those days. We would start pregaming with a few beers at the apartment, and we'd leave our place around 11 p.m. to take the F train into the city to party, carrying a flask in our pockets. By the time we got back from Manhattan, it was 3 a.m., and we'd had at least five or six drinks and spent God knows how much on overpriced whiskey gingers. I think all we ate for two years was Joe's pizza, Bagel World, and Honey Dijon Kettle Chips. Honestly, I'm not sure how we survived back then.

Fast-forward almost fifteen years: if I have two beers, my hangover is so bad, I can't even get out of bed. I haven't really drunk alcohol for the past five years. I'll occasionally have a glass of red wine with a nice meal or champagne at a wedding, but booze doesn't do it for me anymore. I don't like how it makes my body feel, I don't like the way it makes me feel sluggish when I wake up for my morning run or foggy when I try to write.

The good news is that not drinking has helped me deepen relationships with my friends. Instead of doing the requisite "let's go out for drinks," which is predictable and boring, I get to share all kinds of new and exciting experiences with my friends. We go for hikes in the Redwoods. We play Code Names. We cook dinner. We go on bike rides. We go to lectures and poetry readings. We have intimate conversations over cans of Pamplemousse LaCroix. We put on onesies and go to Daybreaker—a sober morning dance party that starts at 7 a.m. on a boat in the San Francisco Bay. I'm not saying that you have to be sober to make new friends, but finding something to do other than drink might make your relationships more fulfilling.

# HOLD SPACE FOR YOUR FRIENDS

As someone with nearly five thousand Facebook friends, I often get made fun of for knowing *too many* people. So does my friend Lani. Lani has been to more than forty weddings (and even officiated four of them!) in recent years, sometimes having a wedding every single month for the entire year. Her friends will often say to her, "Really, *another* wedding, in *November*, in *Ohio*?!"

Not only does Lani know lots of people, she has a special skill for cultivating deep friendships. She intentionally goes deep with people very quickly. She doesn't ask surface questions when she's getting to know somebody, and she has supported other people in opening up and being vulnerable.

This knack for going deep was recently reflected back to Lani at her bachelorette party. Lani had invited thirty-five women for a weekend in the hot springs. She told me, "I know, I know, who the hell has thirty-five women at their bachelorette party?!" Lani's bachelorette was supposed to be in nature but became a virtual bachelorette because of COVID-19.

"I don't like big events or being the center of attention because I like to think about other people," Lani told me. "I was really nervous about the virtual gathering, I hate being on Zoom, and I was thinking that with thirty-five people, it was going to be a total clusterfuck." Instead, the virtual bachelorette was a beautiful celebration of how much Lani had showed up for her friends.

Lani's friends Megan and Shauna facilitated, opening up with a grounding movement exercise so attendees could arrive and be in their bodies, followed by a chance for everyone to answer the question "Who is Lani to you and what do you want to share about what she means in your life?"

Lani told me that, at first, she had a hard time opening up and receiving the love. But she soon realized that she had been on meaningful multiday adventures with every single woman in the room (Zoom). Lani and her friends have been on countless road trips, weekends away, and adventures without distractions. One group of her girlfriends had gotten together for a holiday weekend every single year to eat mushrooms, eat really good food, and go deep together. Lani describes these adventures as times where phones were only used for taking pictures, not for distractions; where there were no to-do lists; and when they got rid of the supposed-tos and were just present with each other.

"I realized that we've shared these moments in time where we were able to hold one another and get into a moment of flow together. We laughed and talked about our lives. We encouraged one another to wonder and be in awe of one another."

Lani's virtual bachelorette served as a special moment to recognize someone who had dedicated much of her adult life to spending time with her friends. Sure, not everyone is going to have thirty-five women at their bachelorette party, but here are a few lessons we can learn from Lani about creating the time and space to go deep with those we care about:

**1. Don't ask surface-level questions.** Lani gets people to open up quickly by asking them personal questions right off the bat. Three of her favorite questions are: *What makes you feel alive? What's the best advice you've* *received lately? What are you excited about in the near future?* By indicating that she's there to hold space for you, she immediately draws people in.

**2. Make reaching out a natural occurrence.** Since college, Lani has lived in Denver, Santa Fe, and Oakland. In every place she's moved and worked, she maintains relationships from the previous places she's lived and cultivates new ones. She doesn't drop people. She makes an effort to reach out to old friends when she's in their town. She calls people on their birthday. When she thinks of someone, she reaches out.

**3. Go on overnight adventures where you have time and space for presence and flow.** Overnight trips and adventures in nature have defined Lani's friendships. They create an environment where people can let their guard down and not be worried about their next meeting or errand or even what time it is. This creates presence and a chance to get into a flow state, where Lani and her friends are fully immersed in the process of being with each other and "holding" each other.

Instead of only going out to restaurants, when you go on an overnight adventure with friends, make meals participatory. Create a meal sign-up sheet and assign everyone one or two meals that they are responsible to shop for and cook. Food is a beautiful way of showing love, and this ritual creates a participatory environment where everyone has to step up and cook for their friends. It also ensures that one person doesn't have to do the shopping or the cooking for the whole group.

**4. Be involved in lots of different groups and activities.** Lani has always been involved in lots of groups and activities like Teach for America, dance team, BBYO youth group, Jewish summer camp; in college, she was part of the Women's Student Assembly and a group called Youth Exploring Passion, which mentored pregnant or parent teens in LA. She's built meaningful relationships from these organizations, and the routines have helped keep the momentum going in her relationships.

# HAVE TEA WITH STRANGERS
# (AND HAVE TEA ALONE)

A few years after I moved to San Francisco, I was feeling bored and a little lonely. A buddy suggested I go to a meet-up called Tea With Strangers. "What's that?" I asked him. "Exactly what it sounds like," he replied. Sure enough, one afternoon I showed up at a beautiful tea house called Samovar and sat with a group of five strangers for two hours. The conversation started with small talk as we all introduced ourselves and moved on to more intentional conversation, led by a volunteer host. The host asked us open-ended questions like "What's something you've been overthinking lately?" and "Tell us about a recent turning point in your life" and "Who's someone in your life that you should say thank-you to?" I remember leaving the event feeling way less bored than when I arrived, like I had met several interesting new people and experienced a very refreshing form of group therapy, all for the very affordable cost of a delicious genmaicha green tea.

Tea With Strangers has now become an international movement, with hosts in fifteen different cities who have invited some fifty thousand strangers to chat for two hours over tea. Ankit Shah, the founder of Tea With Strangers, has hosted more than four hundred of these conversations himself, with more than two thousand strangers. Ankit writes, "What makes a Tea With Strangers conversation meaningful isn't that you just talked with strangers. It's that you have experienced connection with them—that you observed a sense of your Shared Humanity. You just met these people two hours ago, and somehow it feels as though you've known them forever. You've shared stories with them that you forgot even existed, and you've learned things about them that you would've never thought to ask about."

Ankit is on a mission to help people experience their Shared Humanity. Yet, for someone who started a movement to bring strangers together, he is more concerned these days with the opposite side of the coin: making sure people have the tools to be comfortable being alone. When I sat down with Ankit at Souvla, my favorite overpriced salad spot in San Francisco (and there are many overpriced salad spots in San Francisco), he told me that creating spaciousness, curiosity, and awe with strangers can lead to practicing spaciousness, curiosity, and awe with yourself.

In an essay titled "Being Alone," Ankit writes, "Good Alone Time takes practice, and practice can very well be excruciating. As with anything difficult, however, practice makes practice easier. For me, practice is going on long walks in nature—long enough to forget what I was thinking about before I started and instead marvel at how many shades of green there are.

"It's taking a shower before bed to think about my day and leave the water running just long enough to forget that I even had a day in the first place. It's slowly smelling my morning coffee before I start sipping it. It's washing the dishes without my headphones in. It's turning on Airplane Mode and typing out my thoughts to myself as if I'm texting my own consciousness, having a true back-and-forth."

Ankit argues that Good Alone Time can help you get to know who you actually are, help put your life in perspective, learn to enjoy your own company, and, crucially, make connecting with others easier. I find it fascinating that the dude who founded Tea With Strangers five years later is on a mission to help people get more comfortable being alone, in service to actually meeting people in the first place.

Perhaps exploring and uncovering what it's like to spend more time alone—and being *okay* with spending more time alone—is an essential piece of the loneliness puzzle.

Here are five ways to help you ease into creating more Good Alone Time for yourself:

**1. Put alone time on the calendar.** Schedule a regular block of time, on Sunday evening, for example, to be alone. Adding time to be with yourself to your calendar will normalize it and make you look forward to being alone, rather than feeling shame for feeling lonely or feeling like you need to make plans.

**2. Don't be alarmed if it's hard.** As human beings, we're wired to be social animals. Taking time to be with your own thoughts and your own body can often feel like an insurmountable accomplishment. As Jenny Odell writes in *How to Do Nothing*, "Solitude, observation, and simple conviviality should be recognized not as ends in and of themselves, but inalienable rights belonging to anyone lucky enough to be alive. . . . Doing nothing is *hard*."

**3. Spend more time in nature.** A solitary walk outdoors can work wonders. Wandering through nature gives you time to smell the flowers, look up at the trees, listen to the wind, talk to the birds, and stare at the clouds. Wandering through nature gives you time to forget all your push notifications and remind yourself what it's like to be alive on planet Earth and why we need to do everything possible to save our climate.

**4. Ritualize alone time.** Create a playlist to listen to when you're spending time alone. Light a candle. Sit on your favorite pillow. Look out your favorite window. Go on your favorite walk. Make alone time feel special and sacred.

**5. Have tea alone.** Get in the habit of sipping some tea and sitting with yourself. Whether it's meditation, journaling, drawing, or simply just being; you don't need five other people to enjoy your own company and reflect on what makes you *you*. Becoming more comfortable alone takes practice; and the more you practice, the more self-awareness you build, and the more you can flex that Shared Humanity muscle Ankit talks about.

# PRACTICE SHABBAT

My favorite ritual that emerged during the pandemic was practicing Shabbat. Shabbat is the Jewish sabbath, the day of rest, which takes place from Friday evening at sundown until Saturday at sundown. On Shabbat, observant Jews don't use technology, they don't turn on the lights or use the oven, and they don't drive. Shabbat is the old-school digital detox, originating long before cell phones or social media. It's a chance to take a deep breath and pause after a long week of work. I'm Jewish but not observant, yet I felt called to do something special for Shabbat during the pandemic. Shabbat makes me think of being a kid back home in Cambridge, Massachusetts. Even though my family wasn't very religious, we still gathered on Friday night to light candles and eat dinner together, and I loved this ritual to mark the end of the week. After lighting candles, we'd always embrace in a family hug.

When shelter-in-place first started, it seemed like as good a moment as any to start celebrating Shabbat again. At the end of the first week of what would be months of quarantine, I sent out a calendar invite to a small group of friends, seeing if anyone wanted to light Shabbat candles together on Friday evening at 7:30 p.m. on a Zoom call. Our Shabbat ShaZooms grew to as many as forty people, some of whom I had never even met before (and most of whom weren't even Jewish!), and lasted for twelve weeks straight.

Every week, we'd start with a minute of silent reflection. We'd close our eyes and take a few deep breaths. We'd take a moment to be grateful for own presence and our physical health and feel grateful for all of those working hard to keep us safe through such challenging times: the doctors, nurses, and health care workers, the farmers and food delivery workers and grocery clerks. Then we'd sing a song together. I'd ask if anyone wanted to share a prayer for someone who was sick or at-risk. People shared prayers for the elderly, prayers for those locked up behind bars, prayers for those living in refugee camps, and prayers for the homeless. As the weeks went by, people shared prayers for family members giving birth or fighting cancer or friends who had lost their jobs. By April, people were saying prayers for friends who had tested positive for COVID-19, and by May, people were sharing stories of uncles and cousins and neighbors who had died from COVID-19. After these prayers, we lit Shabbat candles together and sang blessings over the wine and bread.

Our entire Shabbat ritual took about twenty minutes, but it was the most meaningful moment of the entire week for me. It was humanizing. It felt like a chance to exhale. I got to see the faces of people I cared about every week. We laughed and smiled and cried. We shared our collective feeling of grief during the pandemic. We also celebrated good news: when someone finished a project at work, or wrote a book, or got a puppy, or Marie Kondo'd their closet, or were finally able to see their parents or grandchildren again after shelter-in-place. Shabbat served as a weekly reminder of how COVID-19 was impacting the daily lives of people I cared about, beyond miserable headlines in the *New York Times* and Donald Trump's repulsive, dehumanizing tweets.

I learned that there is no right way to practice Shabbat. You don't have to be religious, and you don't even have to be Jewish. The only prayer you have to know is who you're thinking about in that moment. It doesn't matter whether people are gathering on Zoom or eating brisket in your mother's dining room. The simple act of slowing down to pause and reflect, to honor the passing of time, to separate the end of one week and the beginning of another, to light candles and celebrate the light in your life, is an exercise that I want to keep incorporating in my life forever.

# BE VULNERABLE
# AROUND OTHER MEN

As I was doing research for this book, most of the books and articles I read about friendship were written by (and for) women. It made me realize that we need a new paradigm in our culture for what a healthy and evolved male friendship can look like. Hollywood's depiction of male friendship is one that often celebrates misogyny and toxic masculinity. (Sorry, *Superbad*. I like Michael Cera and Jonah Hill, but let's be honest here: this movie, like most bro comedies, normalizes rape culture.)

A lack of positive examples of male bonding has serious real-life consequences. In Britain, 2.5 million men admitted to having no close friends. Men conceal pain and illness at much higher rates than women and are three times more likely than women to die from suicide. Systemic racism makes these barriers and mental health challenges even more pronounced for Black men and men of color. We need more models of men being emotionally open and vulnerable with other men. We need more stories of healthy male friend intimacy that are about personal growth and not about trying to get laid.

When my friend Brent Schulkin was thirty-five, he realized that he was lacking a close group of male peers to be open and vulnerable with. Here's what he shared with his close friends:

"I feel like I'm not making enough time for friends. I feel like my role in friendships has become largely reactive, and I've forgotten how to be proactive.

"I feel like inertia plays too large of a role in determining the people I surround myself with, and I want to be more active about curating who I spend time with in acknowledgment of how much we are influenced by those around us.

"I have felt like many of my closest relationships are with women, and I want to bring more gender balance to my inner circle.

"I have realized that my father doesn't have a close-knit group of male friends in the same way that my mother has a close-knit group of female friends, and I've been astonished at how common that is among the fathers of friends I talk to. I presume that I have learned some habits and norms that could put me on a similar path unless I proactively choose a different path.

"I have historically had a shortage of people with whom it feels normal for me to have conversations that are vulnerable, intimate, emotional, or deep. If I need to have conversations like that, I certainly can, but the fact that there is no default space for that or naturally occurring normal time for that means that those sorts of conversations happen less often than they could."

Brent decided to be proactive and start his own men's group. He found a group of six other men—all of whom were friends of his from different parts of his life—and they have met every six to eight weeks for the past four years. They rotate meeting at each other's houses. During every meeting, each person shares what's going on, what they're working on, struggling with, or whatever else is present for them. Each meeting starts with dinner, and then they do a short meditation to get grounded. After that, everyone spends five to fifteen minutes sharing what's going on in their lives. After each person's check-in, there is a follow-up question or two before moving on to the next person. After the check-ins, they have a group discussion about a theme that has been chosen for the evening—whomever hosts chooses the theme. Discussion themes have included communication with romantic partners and parents, building good habits and accountability, and deep questions like "What makes you feel the most alive?" and "If you could start all over, what would you do differently?"

Here are a few guiding principles the group uses to build intimacy, as shared by Brent:

**Confidentiality:** Sharing your own experience outside of the group is okay, but don't tell anyone about what other people share.

**Practice vulnerability:** Men, in particular, need practice in this area. Confidentiality creates a safe space for this. The level of vulnerability has gotten noticeably higher after a couple years of getting to know one another.

**No judgment:** "Notice judgments that arise, hold them lightly, question them, or let them go," as someone in the group says. Sure, it's virtually impossible to avoid judgment altogether, but practice doesn't hurt.

**Don't try to fix it without consent:** Actually, most of us really like it when others try to fix something, and that helps us get a lot out of the experience. But sometimes this is not what is needed, so it's important to check before jumping in with solutions, as we men are so often prone to do.

The structure is simple, but Brent said that the group has had a profound impact on his life. "It is men in this culture who have a much harder time with friendship, and it is men who most urgently need to practice ways of relating that seem to come much more easily to women in this culture," he said. "It has given me an increased sense of routine and stability that I think was missing from my experience of friendship."

Dozens of men I spoke to shared similar challenges of cultivating male friendship as an adult. One of my friends and favorite speakers,

Ashanti Branch, has made it his life's work to help men become more in touch with their emotions at a young age. Ashanti is the founder and executive director of the Ever Forward Club in Oakland, California, which started as a safe space for underserved and at-risk young men of color to talk about what's going on in their lives without worry of feeling ashamed and now serves young men of all backgrounds.

When Ashanti was a dean at his former high school, Fremont High School, in Oakland, California, he realized that a lot of the boys and teenagers he was working with were saying everything in their lives was going fine while, in reality, things were much darker. Ashanti helped these young men take off the masks they were wearing and share common feelings of pain, loss, lack of self-worth, lack of love, fear, loneliness, anxiety, depression, and anger. Ashanti's work to help young men become more vulnerable and be able to cope with these emotions was featured in Jennifer Siebel Newsom's Netflix documentary *The Mask You Live In*, about boys and young men struggling to find themselves within America's narrow definition of masculinity.

If you want to start or join a men's group or learn more about the modern masculinity movement, check out the online Resources Guide at smileyposwolsky.com/friendship.

# UPLIFT OTHER WOMEN

Many of the women I interviewed for this book told me that they were part of a women's group that was an essential part of their social life. Ilana Lipsett, Alanna Mednick, and thirteen of their female friends have been meeting monthly since 2012. Their women's circle was born out of a desire to have a more ritualistic space, where womxn could come together and support each other. The guiding mission is "You got this, we got you." It was inspired by one of the circle member's mothers, who has been in a women's circle for more than thirty years.

Every month, whoever is celebrating their birthday that month hosts the circle, and folks who can't make it in person call in via video conference. Someone opens with a welcome and grounding meditation, and the host chooses the theme for that circle, usually in the form of a question for reflection like "What would you like to leave behind this year?" or "What resources do you want to offer in this time of civil uprising and fighting for racial justice?" Each person does an uninterrupted share about whatever is present for them, and others are invited to simply listen to the person sharing. At the end of the share, listeners ask, "Is there anything you need right now?" In order to stay connected between meetings, the circle has a WhatsApp group, where members can share a highlight or challenge, make a request for support or guidance, or offer a social invitation.

It's a simple format that creates permission for participants to share in a confidential space without the fear of being judged and then listen without feeling pressure to fix someone else or solve their problems with the "right" advice. Ilana and Alanna both expressed how present they felt in the company of their women's circle and how the monthly meetings had led to stronger friendships and deeper connection.

"It provides a strong sense of community and connection that is often lacking in daily interactions," Alanna told me. "I've been able to see my growth over the months and years and see the growth in others. It's such a safe space to hear what people are going through, where you can be comfortable sharing the inner workings of your heart and brain, to feel like I can be authentically vulnerable in that space. It normalized my emotions and feelings, to see that everyone is going through something, behind the scenes of all the social media stuff, to see what's really going on. It makes me feel validated."

"Facebook and Instagram have depersonalized relationships, with people broadcasting major life updates to the entire world every second," Ilana added. "In women's circle, we witness people's lives unfold more intimately, and I get to be witnessed by womxn I trust and respect. Whether it's breakups, babies, health issues, marriages, engagements, losing parents; to be so close to all those things is a part of the human experience that we don't often get, and it creates a deeper sense of meaning in these relationships."

I asked Ilana and Alanna if they had any advice for womxn looking to create their own women's circle. Here are four things they shared:

**1. Make your intentions known.** If you're looking for other womxn to join you, let the world know what you're creating and who you're looking for. Chances are, you'll find at least a few inspiring womxn who want to join the circle. Send an email to people you know, post on Facebook or Nextdoor, talk to coworkers, and spread the word.

**2. Start with values and norms.** Ask your fellow circle members what they want to get out of the experience, and discuss what you all need to create a safe, inclusive, confidential, and welcoming space. Decide whether it feels better to keep the circle closed to new members—so participants really get to know each other and trust each other—or if you want to allow new members to join, and what the process is for adding new people to the circle.

**3. Add some structure, but don't overprogram.** Be open-minded about the process. You might need less structure or programmed activities than you think. There is a simple power in coming together and sharing. Figure out what feels natural for the group in terms of how often you'll be meeting and who will be hosting (or whether it will be online or via video if participants live far apart), and consider sharing facilitation responsibilities so it's not too much work for one person. Come up with a plan for how you'll stay connected and communicate, like a WhatsApp group, Slack channel, or Facebook group.

**4. Lift up other womxn.** We don't spend enough time advocating for our friends' personal and professional success. "For womxn specifically, our culture is so much about tearing womxn down and picking apart every inch of her being and her body," Ilana said. "Womxn need a sacred group of sisters lifting them up instead of tearing them down, supporting them instead of shaming them, and allowing them to exist in their femininity instead of hiding it."

"The world would be a better place if everyone had a women's circle or men's circle or just a person's circle, where they can express what they are going through and be held in this way," Alanna added. "Because of the nature of our world, we need to make sure womxn have these safe spaces."

# START A MONDAY NIGHT ACTIVITY CLUB

When I lived in Washington, DC, I found it hard to meet people I really liked spending time with. Everyone seemed so obsessed with politics, and I wanted to talk about something else. That was until I discovered a little unofficial meet-up group called Monday Night Activity Club, started by my friend Gayle Abrams. Monday Night Activity Club, or MNAC as we called it, was where I met my closest friends in DC.

As Gayle recalls, "I was living in DC, teaching fourth grade, and wanting more connection with people I wasn't teaching concepts of fractions to. I wanted to dance and laugh and play. Monday Night Activity Club was born. Word spread, and before I knew it, I had made friends with some of the best, smartest, and most talented people."

The premise was simple: get together with a few nerdy people on a Monday night and hang out. Each week, the activity would be led by a different group member. We played ultimate Frisbee in Malcolm X Park, capture the flag on the National Mall, had arts and crafts night, potluck dinners, did beatboxing and yoga ball soccer, and sometimes we just sat and read books together. I always knew I could look forward to seeing a few good folks on Monday evenings.

On one of our most memorable Mondays, Gayle snuck home her classroom projector, and fifteen of us took over her roommate's bedroom, as our friend Hayley led us in learning the dance count to the "Call Your Girlfriend" music video by Robyn. Nearly ten years later, spread across the country and sheltering-in-place due to COVID-19, we organized an MNAC Zoom reunion so we could dance to Robyn together again—Gayle called it "Zoom Your Girlfriend."

"I was lonely, but I don't enjoy drinking as a mechanism for fun, and 'play' for adults often looks like happy hour or any activity wrapped up in alcohol," remembers Gayle. "I was craving genuine connections with other people who truly enjoyed having fun through play in the childlike sense and who were willing to engage in activities that were unfamiliar and even a bit uncomfortable. It was through learning *new* things that we formed real friendships. And it was also cool to see how different kinds of activities—yoga ball soccer, tag, wiffle ball, poetry, eighties' aerobic dance night, etc.—interested different people. Anytime someone new showed up, I made a point to get to know them. I would ask, 'How did you find out about us?' and 'Would you like to lead an activity? What do you like to do that other people might enjoy learning?'"

It was important to Gayle that MNAC was free and accessible to anyone and that it wasn't ever exclusive. She never posted about it on social media, but as people showed up for activities and realized how special it was, it became a topic of conversation at parties and potlucks. Over time, the MNAC Google Group grew to more than three hundred people. "The listserv literally became a community tool," says Gayle. "It was used to communicate about MNAC activities as well as housing needs and other events happening around the city."

Try hosting a Monday (or Tuesday!) Night Activity Club in your city. Start with a few people you know, or post the event on Facebook, Eventbrite, or Meetup. There are an infinite number of activities you could do together, but here are a few to get you started:

Go for a bike ride
Make pottery
Paint a mural
Sip tea
Start a book club
Play authentic connection games
Do improv
Meditate
Play Dungeons & Dragons
Cook a meal
Hold your local officials accountable
Take a sound bath
Write poems
Sing
Plant herbs
Run for local office
Journal
Play a board game
Film a music video
Dance to Robyn
Listen to each other tell stories
Record a podcast
Volunteer in your community
Host a fund-raiser
Register people to vote

# MAKE AN ALL MY
# FRIENDS PLAYLIST

Have you ever made a list of all the places you've ever lived, the people who have changed your life in each of those places, and the songs that make you think of those special people? I hadn't either until my friend Catherine Woodiwiss from MNAC inspired me to create an All My Friends Playlist.

Catherine was moving to Austin after living in Washington, DC, for nine years, and she commemorated the move by making a Spotify playlist that she posted on Facebook. Her playlist was broken up into nine different chapters from her time in DC, and each of the chapters featured the songs that made Catherine remember special friends from that time in her life. She titled the playlist "DC: This Makes Me Think of You."

"Turns out, when you play music in a place for nearly a decade, and you're sense memory–minded, and you're especially music-associative, a bunch of these moments pile up," Catherine wrote. "I started this list on a whim—jotting down specific songs I learned from you, rearranged with you, road-tripped to with you, danced to with you, worked to with you, saw in concert with you, sang with you, sang to you—and wound up with nearly 70 people-song associations. DC folk, for each of these songs that always make me think of each of you: thanks for prompting the creation of this extremely nostalgic, cheesy soundtrack to an extremely wonderful nine years. <3."

For the record, my song on Catherine's list was from chapter 3: 2011, and it was "Midnight City" by M83. When I saw that post, it took me back to late-night dance parties at our friends' house; the Jamjar on Lamont Street in Washington, DC; dancing to "Midnight City" with Catherine and our friends Gayle, Ann, Meredith, Abe, Fanfoni, and Nate. Those memories brought me so much joy. I immediately put "Midnight City" on my stereo and had a solo dance party in my bedroom.

So, what are you waiting for? Make a list of the different chapters of your life. Then, make a list of the people who most shaped you during those chapters and the songs that make you remember the best moments with the friends you love most. If you feel inspired, share your playlist with them.

# HAVE AN INTENTIONAL BACHELOR (OR BACHELORETTE) PARTY

When people think of a group of men getting together to celebrate their buddy who is getting married, the first thing that usually comes to mind is getting drunk and going to a strip club in Las Vegas. Las Vegas is probably my least favorite place on the planet, and I'm lucky to surround myself with men who feel the same way.

For my best friend Milo's bachelor party two years ago, we gathered the closest men in his life for an intentional celebration of friendship at the beach along the Sonoma coast. Milo loves to draw, so he bought each of us his favorite pen—a Micron drawing pen—and we spent an hour drawing a mural together. Then all of us got naked, walked into the bosom of the Pacific Ocean, and interlocked arms so the waves wouldn't knock us over. Yes, his bachelor party consisted of eight dudes naked on the beach, drawing with Micron pens and painting with watercolors. It was rowdy. Afterward, we went around in a circle sharing what we loved about Milo. Then Milo got to share what he loved about each of us. Later that night, we screened *The Big Lebowski* on the side of a barn, chilled in a hot tub, and had a dance party until three in the morning. It was a magical night.

For my best friend Dre's bachelor party, his boys kayaked across Tomales Bay, north of Point Reyes, California, and camped out for two nights on a remote beach miles away from other people. It's always fascinated me how many people celebrate a bachelor party at a bar or a nightclub. Why would I want to spend time with one of my brothers in a dark, crowded place, surrounded by strangers? Two nights on Pita Beach gave the six of us ample time away from civilization, away from any other humans, in a beautiful and safe setting, to play.

We ran around naked in the sun. We stared up at the clouds. We kayaked under the moon and the stars. We buried our shit in the woods. We tried speaking to the egrets. We stared into the campfire and told every story from college we could remember. We quoted *Seinfeld* and *The Big Lebowski* ad nauseam. We fell over from laughing so hard. We sang "This Must Be the Place (Naïve Melody)" by Talking Heads at the top of our lungs. When it got cold out, in order to stay warm, the six of us embraced each other in a big pig pile for what felt like an eternity—it could have been five minutes or fifty minutes—I can't really say. It was a spiritual experience of oneness and brotherhood. These days, when the Pita Beach crew reunites for weekly Zoom calls, we catch up about what's going on with our jobs and families, but we inevitably spend half the call having flashbacks about our time on Tomales Bay.

Next time you plan a bachelor party, think about what you can do that really represents the human you're honoring. How can you love your buddy for what makes him *him*? How can you express—emotionally express—what your friend means to you? Challenge yourself to create an intentional and truly memorable experience.

# THINK LIKE A CHIEF EXPERIENCE OFFICER

If Life were a company, Levi Felix would have been its Chief Experience Officer. He was meticulous when it came to experience design and ritual (a personality trait that sometimes bordered on obsession), and he never missed an opportunity to architect a transformational experience. At Camp Grounded, Levi would spend hours walking around the redwoods with the production team at night, making sure each tree was perfectly lit and would make someone feel the magical power of being in nature. When campers received their welcome packets and their village assignments for camp, they were also greeted with an envelope full of glitter that spilled everywhere, making a huge mess.

When you were with Levi, you didn't just eat dinner, you first burned your deepest fear—the one thing that was standing in the way of you living a more authentic life—and then you sat on a picnic blanket by candlelight, with 350 other people in silence, among the redwoods, under the stars, dressed all in white, while someone played the sitar.

When you were with Levi, the mundane tasks that make up most of our daily lives—eating, having a conversation, taking a walk—turned into deep moments of intention, reflection, and gratitude. And wonderful opportunities to mess with people. The ultimate trickster, nothing gave Levi more pleasure than messing with people's reality or making people question the world around them.

When you were with Levi at Burning Man, he'd make you schlep thirty-pound suitcases of sushi and sake out to the middle of the desert. The whole time you'd be thinking, "Why the hell are we lugging raw fish out to the middle of the desert?!" Because Levi thought it'd be cool to have a three-hour dinner ceremony at two o'clock in the morning.

One time we were out on the playa on an art car adventure, and Levi started introducing our "Zen as Fuck" crew to another Burner. The introduction took twenty minutes. "My name is Professor Fidget Wigglesworth," he began. "I have several advanced degrees in digital detoxification, philosophy, and Earth studies. This is my partner-in-love, Bruce. This is my brother and senior associate, Mobius. This is Moose, Smiley, Barnaby, Smokey, and KJ . . . we're out here looking for the answer to the universe—and my drum set, which I can't seem to find."

The other Burner looked at Levi like he was completely nuts and said, "Well, my name's Rob and I'm drunk."

We stayed up all night running around the playa like kids in a candy store and watched the sun rise over Black Rock Desert with our friends. Just after the sunrise, we saw a school bus drive by, and wouldn't you know it, Levi's drum kit was on it. I think we also found the answer to the universe, which was, quite simply: just spend more time with your friends.

# Forty Fun Rituals to Practice with Your Friends

**If you're struggling to come up with some of your own friendship rituals, here are a few to inspire you:**

Ashley Rose Hogrebe, founder of Do the Damn Thing, a business service that helps feminist creatives get organized and accountable so they can achieve their goals, hosts **You Did It!**—a party to celebrate nontraditional milestones. Participants gather to celebrate things like starting a business, landing your first partnership, booking your first client, raising your rates, rebranding, finding a therapist, or whatever you want.

Melissa Wong hosts **Messy Circles**, a place where you can embrace being unfinished and unpolished and less alone during the messy parts of life. Messy Circles are supportive gatherings where a small group of humans gets together to share any messy thoughts or feelings present and enter into a brave space where mess is welcomed with open arms.

Jillian Richardson sends out **notes of being awesome**. Whenever she's in a conversation and talks about how awesome someone is, she pauses and sends them a message right then to let them know how awesome they are. As Jillian says, "I never know what mental state someone is in when I send them that random love, and I often receive messages back like 'I was really struggling. I needed that.'"

Friends Nathalie Arbel and Hunter Franks used to send each other a **good-night text** before going to bed. Kind of like when your parents used to read *Goodnight Moon* to you when you were a little kid, it's nice to get a good-night wish from a friend.

Nathalie's mom and her three close friends, who are all European immigrants in their sixties, have an annual **women's weekend**. Once a year for thirty years, they've planned a weekend getaway, and they've managed to keep up their weekends from back when they met in California, through having full-time jobs and raising multiple children.

Anna Akullian and her friend Gina have a **November 17 phone call**. They made a pact when they were best friends in seventh grade to always talk on November 17, and they've kept it for seventeen years and counting.

Anthony Scopatz and Jana Hirsch host **odd Fridays**. On odd Fridays, they have a potluck at a friend's house, and all you have to do is show up as you are.

My parents took a summer camping trip they deemed **adventure before dementia**. When they turned sixty-two years old, they got a Lifetime Senior Pass to America's National Parks, which only cost ten dollars at the time. My mom and dad drove across the country and stopped to hike and camp in the Rocky Mountains, Bryce Canyon, Arches, Sequoia, and Kings Canyon National Parks. They ended their trip—looking as youthful as ever—meeting my sister and me in Yosemite National Park.

Erin Kim created **Lettres Mag**, a print magazine of love letters from around the world, conceived from a desire to revitalize modern connection.

Kat Vellos wrote **Connected from Afar**, a collection of prompts and conversation starters for bringing depth to your friendships, even if you are far away. One of my favorites is "Yelp Review," where they write a Yelp review about each other as if it would be read by a stranger who was considering becoming a friend with them.

Patrick Ip and Christine Lai host **baller dinners** in cities all across the country. Baller dinners are curated, multigenerational, and interdisciplinary dinner parties of eight to fifteen interesting people, where everyone contributes to the cost of dinner. Ballers believe in action over talk, humility over arrogance, and inclusion over exclusion. Dinner attendees are encouraged to share their story, check their ego at the door, and always ask, "How can I help?"

Every single night, Mel Brooks drove from Santa Monica to Beverly Hills to chat, **eat dinner, and watch Jeopardy!** with his friend of seventy years, fellow actor and comedian Carl Reiner. Carl passed away in 2020, but as Mel said, "This is a great place because I got friendship, love, and free food. Free eats are very important."

My friend Sara Weinberg is a treasure chest when it comes to friend rituals. Here are a few of her favorites. **Trips for tacos:** you give someone a ride to the airport (or help them move or do them a favor), and in return, they take you out for tacos. Instead of a financial reward or a physical gift, the exchange means even more friend time.

**Signature greeting:** Sara and a friend invent a hug/greeting neither has ever done before and it becomes their signature greeting, a playful and fun way to see her friends, especially since her love language is physical touch.

**Romantic friend dates:** Sara takes friends out on a not-so-cheesy date. "Why do you have to be 'romantic' with just a partner?" she wonders. She gives her friend flowers, dresses up, buys them dinner, and even surprises them. During coronavirus, she even did this a few times on Zoom.

For a remote ritual, Sara practices **Facebook memory lane:** she and a friend share their screens and take turns picking random old Facebook pictures of one another and have each person explain the context of the picture.

Lastly, Sara and a friend come up with **joint yearly intentions**. Last year's theme was "Big Joy," and that theme informed everything they did. Every time they inter-acted, they tried to bring some element of Big Joy, which means making the person beam with a huge smile or having them laugh uncontrollably or whatever fills their happy cup in that moment.

Ankit Shah started the **Silent Hike Society** to bring a small group of people together for long, silent hikes in nature followed by a conversation over lunch.

Liz Travis Allen and her friends have a **virtual cooking club** to cook recipes together when they are far apart. During quarantine, they read Samin Nosrat's cookbook, *Salt Fat Acid Heat*, and used the app MarcoPolo to share short videos of the food they were cooking.

To catch up with each other, frequent travelers and friends Liz and James have a recurring **where are you now?** calendar invitation. Each year, on September 12, they have a phone call to see where their friend is and how the past year has been.

Every summer for the past thirteen years, Liz's parents, Dean and Susan, who are in their sixties, host a monthly **full moon kayak** and invite their friends to kayak in the San Francisco Bay at night.

Fred, seventy-two, and Linda, sixty, host **Friendsgiving in June** at their home in Lake George, New York. When they moved to the lake nine years ago, they didn't know anyone, but they began befriending people through their real estate agent. The first Friendsgiving brought twelve people together, and now more than thirty people come every year. Many attendees say it's their favorite event of the year. Friendsgiving in June even has its own logo: a turkey sitting in an Adirondack chair, wearing hiking boots.

Kasley and her friend host a **narrative night**. Instead of bringing wine, guests are told to bring a personal story related to a theme; for example, one theme was "Recent Revelation." After using conversation prompts to break the ice, strangers share their story in a supportive environment.

Mark Brenner, seventy-one, and his best friend Buzz, sixty-seven, are in a **breakfast club** together. Every year for fifteen years, they have met up at 8:56 a.m. (to beat the 9:00 a.m. crowd) at a local breakfast joint. They generally spend two and a half hours talking about relationships, family, work, politics, and, in Mark's words, "our Seinfeldian, meshuganah, curmudgeonly notions about other humans."

Lauren Cohen Fisher's **annual canoe trip** in Maine with the same group of friends since 2015 has taught her that friendships generate rituals but also that rituals generate friendships. Something magical happens hours from phone service, paddling through hurricanes, mosquito infestations, and beautiful sunsets.

Lauren also has a standing **Tuesday lunch date** with three best friends. They bike from their respective offices and eat together for an hour. The time has become holy, blocked out like any other important meeting.

When Lauren and a friend are upset, they sometimes write **anonymous letters** to people they find in the phone book.

Matt and his buddies have **pancake Saturdays** after going surfing together in the morning.

Every morning, Maggie and her friends have a **gratitude practice**, where they text the group thread one thing they are grateful for.

The early employees at Good Eggs, an organic grocery delivery company based in the Bay Area, used to have a **Tuesday night team dinner**. They all went to the farmers' market to buy groceries and then cooked together.

Michael Liskin, Rebecca, Beth, and a group of twenty friends have an annual **New Year's Day gathering**. They meet up with their friends and friends' kids. At sunset, they all walk down to Venice Beach to see the sunset and talk about their visions for the year ahead.

Every day for an entire year, Dev and his friend Lisa texted each other a photo. At the end of the year, they printed a **photo book** with all of their photos from the year.

During university, Dev and his friend Mimi gave each other a set of **addressed and stamped postcards** to make it easier to write each other. Twelve years after getting the set, Dev found one of the last remaining postcards in his desk and sent it to Mimi for a pleasant surprise.

Every holiday season for the past eight years, Lani and forty of her friends and family have had a **white elephant costume exchange** on the winter solstice as a way to bring light and play into the darkest time of year. Everyone is told to bring a costume and wrap it. Each person gets a number, and whatever costume you get, you have to put it on and embody the character. "It's an activity not just a party," Lani says. "You get to see your friends and be weird together." Lani's friend Sebastian, a DJ, finds a song to match each costume, and every person does a cat walk in the middle of the room so they can have their moment.

Jenny Yrasuegui and a group of seven girlfriends participate in a **communal birthday gift** ritual. Instead of giving individual gifts, everyone in the group throws in thirty dollars, and the birthday celebrant gets to feel special and pick something nice she wants for her birthday.

Josh Kelley and their roommate indulge in a weekly **decompression** exercise together. First, they sit on the porch, share a joint, and philosophize in the way that only two stoned friends could possibly do. Then, they order food from one of their favorite neighborhood restaurants and enjoy dinner together while binge-watching a TV series. The ritual doesn't conclude until they've motivated each other to get off the couch, brush their teeth together, chat about the show they just watched, and finally say good night.

A group of Josh's friends started a monthly **documentary club** ("a book club for lazy people"). For

over a year and a half, they have met once a month to share wine, snacks, and a documentary they want to see. In the era of social distancing, they started with a Zoom catch-up call before hopping over to a Netflix party to watch the documentary together.

Every summer, Josh gets together with a bunch of their fellow LGBTQ friends to go on vacation together. Josh loves their **gay-cation** ritual. Usually, they hit up destinations with a rich history for the LGBTQ community, like Provincetown and Fire Island. For a weekend or a whole week, they just hang out on the beach, drink, dance, party, and "participate in the magic that is a hetero-free, pride-full weekend of being ourselves and celebrating what makes us unique and special." As Josh says, "It's a queer takeover of paradise, and for a moment the world is ours and ONLY ours."

Joanna has a letter-writing ritual called **Everything I Never Said**. She picks a friend who's on her mind and shares with them all the things she thinks of them, admires about them, the memories she has of them that she wants the friend to know.

Joanna also **saves voicemails** to Google Drive because she wants to have artifacts of people she loves and, in her words, "There might be a time when I don't get to hear their voice again."

# PART SIX

# Be a Minister for Loneliness in Your Community

# BE AN AGENT OF
# HUMAN CONNECTION

After a 2017 report was published by the Jo Cox Commission on Loneliness, indicating that more than nine million people in Britain often or always feel lonely, then–prime minister Theresa May appointed a Minister for Loneliness to help with the problem. Research by the British government had found that some two hundred thousand older people in Britain had not had a conversation with a friend or relative in more than a month. While other countries will hopefully follow suit, we can't wait for public institutions to solve the loneliness epidemic for us. We each need to become a Minister for Loneliness in our own community.

My friend Ivan Cash is an award-winning interactive artist, filmmaker, speaker, and connection agent who's all about coming up with proactive ways to connect people in real life. Ivan wrote a book, called *Snail Mail My Email,* based on a worldwide collaborative art project where volunteers "translate" strangers' emails into written letters and mail them to their intended recipients free of charge. Here are just a few of the fun, creative projects he's deployed in the past few years to get you inspired:

**Last Photo Project:** Ivan started by asking people on the streets of San Francisco to share the last photo on their phone and the story behind the photo. Since launching in San Francisco, the video project has spread to the streets of Los Angeles, Miami, Detroit, New York, Honolulu, and London, and has been viewed more than a million times. As Ivan says, "Each film captures the essence of the city's cultural zeitgeist while revealing intimate candid peeks into its inhabitants' lives. Everyday trivialities, triumphs, and tragedies documented through our phones are exposed, showing our shared humanity."

**Strangers Drawing Strangers:** In this project, Ivan works with Airbnb at the Sundance Film Festival. Sundance attendees get a Polaroid picture of themselves taken and then put their photo in a huge file cabinet. A stranger selects a photo from the cabinet and draws that person on a piece of paper with colored pencils and markers. All the portraits are put up on the wall in the exhibition space—another simple way of bringing people just a little bit closer together.

**Agent of Connection:** In this three-minute documentary film, Ivan profiles William Cromartie, a Bay Area Rapid Transit (BART) employee in Oakland, California, who is not your average subway station agent. William actually engages with and says hello to the people who pass by his BART station booth, interacting with hundreds of strangers on a daily basis. "Every day that I come to work, I engage with four thousand people," William explains in the film. "I speak to them, I say hello, I invite them in, I give them good graces going out, I fist bump, I shake hands; people that I have an established relationship with, I hug. I'm not a booth troll, I stay outside; that's where the people are. . . . Being able to look out and see the world as it is—the homeless, the hurt, the happy, the focused, the different walks of life that I engage in—it's all beautiful. I'm happy to be a part of it. Stepping forward and saying hello to someone and occupying someone else's space and learning about that person is the easiest and the best thing in the world. I could do this every day."

William's story reminds us of the simple but powerful act of saying hello. I love his story and all of Ivan's projects, because they remind us that you don't need to be appointed by the prime minister to become a Minister for Loneliness. Wherever you go—on an airplane, on the subway, on the street—think about ways you might look up from your phone and talk to strangers. We all need to become better agents of human connection.

# SPEND MORE TIME WITH PEOPLE WHO ARE OLDER (AND WISER) THAN YOU

There's something incredibly refreshing about older people because they don't have to prove their brilliance to you. A lot of millennials I know (and I'll include myself in this category) can be a little self-important. Many millennials walk around like, "Hey, I wrote a book! I started a company! I'm a founder! I'm a *Forbes* 30 Under 30! I'm smart! I have followers! People love me on Instagram! I matter! I swear I matter!"

A lot of people in their sixties, seventies, and eighties are simply just cool as f*ck. They don't need to remind you all the time.

I once attended a conference where I was one of the youngest people in the room. I kept having conversations with people who, from their bios, I knew had published eight books, started three companies, failed at starting two companies, worked for two large organizations, traveled the world, painted, written poetry, *and* raised two kids—and yet, when they introduced themselves, were curious about my story and what they could learn from me. I kept meeting accomplished businesswomen who were quick to point out everything they didn't know yet and wanted to learn. I met academics who were at the top of their field, some of the most brilliant people alive, and who attended panels and asked questions as if they were in elementary school.

Most millennials and Gen-Zers I know don't do this.

Being in the presence of such accomplished individuals (many of whom also moonlight as gardeners, poets, painters, opera singers, theater buffs, botanists, parents, and grandparents) was humbling, to say the least. The event taught me that the true purpose of life is not to find your purpose, as so many young people I meet seem to be obsessed with doing (damn all those millennial self-help authors nicknamed Smiley!). The true purpose of life is to never stop learning. To always surround yourself with people who aren't your age, people who know things you don't know, people who don't necessarily share your opinions, and people who make you question the world around you.

Find an event to attend where you will be one of the youngest people in the room. Not simply a space where people who are cool can congregate to talk about how cool they are. Not simply a space to get recognition for something you know is already great from people who already think you are great. But a place where you challenge your worldview, where you learn from others older than you, and where people from different backgrounds can openly and honestly come together and talk about the things that are not easy to talk about.

# FOSTER
# INTERGENERATIONAL
# FRIENDSHIPS

In June 2020, nearly four months into the COVID-19 pandemic, I was introduced to my partner's great aunt Deb. Aunt Deb—Deborah Berlinger Eiferman—is ninety-seven years old and lives on the Hudson River north of New York City. My partner told me that Aunt Deb had watched my TED talk and wanted to meet me. "I'm too old to fall in love," she said. "But, Adam, I fell in love with your words when I watched your TED talk." What a sweet thing to say.

Aunt Deb went on to tell me that she was the happiest she had ever been in her life. "I'm on three Zooms a day," she explained. "I'm listening to music. I'm writing a book. I'm taking a Bible class. A breath, body, and mind class. I'm going to concerts without having to arrange for transportation."

The pandemic had given Aunt Deb the ability to connect with the world and keep learning without having to leave the house—something that isn't easy when you're ninety-seven. I was struck by Aunt Deb's positive outlook, especially since her sister's husband had just passed away from COVID a few weeks before. "This is my third epidemic," Aunt Deb told me, describing her experiences surviving scarlet fever when she was five and then living through the polio epidemic. "I'm one grateful aunt. I feel very positive about aging."

When Deb's husband of more than sixty-four years, Irving Eiferman, died in 2012, she made a pact to make friends only with people younger than she was. There's evidence that intergenerational connection reduces ageism in both directions. It gives people positive perceptions of generations and contributes to better health and longevity. It can inspire younger people to care more about aging, to learn from elders, and it encourages people to explore careers in service and caregiving and volunteerism.

"Someone who connects with different generations is being more socially active, and that engagement promotes healthy aging," says Kasley Killam, who received her master's in public health at the Harvard School of Public Health and specializes in social health and solutions for the loneliness epidemic. "Intergenerational friendship engenders a sense of purpose and meaning no matter your age. It's valuable for older adults who've lost their social networks at work and may be isolated for the first time; it's a way to stay involved and contribute. And younger people can learn from elders' experiences and perspectives."

The intergenerational friendship movement has been gaining momentum for some time. Data have shown that young people ages sixteen to twenty-four are the most likely demographic to report feeling lonely and that although loneliness decreases as adults get older—perhaps as we learn to become more intentional and selective in our relationships—it increases again once people reach seventy-five.

There are so many great programs and organizations out there to help foster these relationships. For example, the Intergenerational Learning Center, established in Seattle in 1991, offers programs for children at a place that is also home to more than four hundred older adults. Five days a week, the children and residents come together in a variety of planned activities, such as music, dancing, art, lunch, storytelling, or just visiting. The platform Nesterly tackles the challenge of housing affordability and aging in place by providing "intergenerational homesharing," allowing elderly homeowners the chance to rent out extra rooms in their home to gain some much-needed company (and even make some extra money). CIRKEL closes the generational gap by connecting you to someone from a different age group for career and life advice. The nonprofit organization Encore helps retirees offer their skills and expertise in a fellowship program, offering stipend-paid "encore careers." Gen2Gen is Encore's campaign to mobilize one million adults who are over fifty to stand up for—and with—young people; they've built partnerships with more than 250 organizations, developed best practices for engaging older adults in nonprofit work, and provided mini-grants to activists.

During quarantine, Aunt Deb's synagogue connected her with an eighteen-year-old woman named Tali Safran, who had recently graduated from high school in New Jersey. Tali was feeling a little bored with her classmates and wanted to do something to help out during coronavirus, so she asked a teacher if she could talk to an older person. Aunt Deb and Tali started talking twice a week on the phone, found it mutually beneficial, and enjoyed it so much that they decided to meet in person during COVID (safely, of course) on Aunt Deb's outdoor terrace.

Aunt Deb also joined a faith group begun by her synagogue that organized intergenerational groups of eight people to call each other once a week during quarantine. Every Friday, her neighbors—a younger couple—came over (with masks on) to bring her long-stem roses. Aunt Deb was hard at work on her third book, titled *My Lucky Stroke*, about finding gratitude and appreciation no matter what life throws at you.

Aunt Deb was clearly living her best life *at ninety-seven years old during a pandemic*, thanks in part to the intergenerational connection in her life. I asked Kasley to share her favorite tips on fostering more intergenerational friendships in your life.

**1. Plug in.** Chances are there's a nonprofit in your city that offers community programs for older adults and neighbors. Google it. They've already done the work, so start by seeing what existing opportunities you can plug into.

**2. Volunteer.** This should be required for everyone! When you volunteer—for whatever cause it might be—you organically form intergenerational friendships and meet people of all ages doing something you mutually care about. It's a great way to form connections and gain a sense of meaning and purpose.

**3. Reach out.** Call your grandparents! Or your great aunt (or your partner's great aunt!). Simple acts of connection are underrated. Leave a note in your neighbor's mailbox. Knock on the door of an older neighbor (with a mask on). Organize a six-feet-apart potluck on Nextdoor. Think local. Each of us has a family and friends and neighbors with whom we can deepen our relationships. It doesn't have to be a dramatic initiative; it's about taking one action.

**4. Use conversation as an anchor.** People want to share their story. People want to open up about the real stuff they are going through. Give them a space to do that. Host intimate gatherings. Share first so that others feel comfortable sharing. Otherwise, it's too easy to fall back on talking about the weather and politics.

# CREATE A SUPPORT SYSTEM FOR NEW PARENTS

When I posted on Facebook that I was writing a book about friendship, I got lots of likes and heart emojis as dozens of friends commented with enthusiastic notes of celebration like "Can't wait to read this book, Smiley!" But the comment that stuck with me the most was far more somber. My friend, whom I'll call Adele, wrote that she was feeling really affected reading my post as a new parent. She had a lot of trouble maintaining friendships while being a mom. She said the isolation of new parenthood was so acute and made even worse by social media, since parenting groups and listservs provided the illusion of connection when they really don't scratch that true friendship itch.

As hard as it is for all adults to maintain friendships, it's even harder for new parents. We don't talk enough about the toll of parenthood—especially of motherhood—on our friends and family members. Cleveland Clinic estimates that as many as 50 to 75 percent of new mothers experience the "baby blues" after delivery, and one in seven women will develop a more severe and longer-lasting depression after delivery, called *postpartum depression*.

"It's incredibly hard in ways that are difficult to express," Adele commented on my post. "I had postpartum depression after my first child and decided for the second time around to start seeing a therapist while I was pregnant. It has made an enormous difference. Also, I'm trying to unplug more so that nursing/time with baby and toddler are focused, quality time. Otherwise, I can get lost adrift in social media, feeling like I'm missing out on something that I can't put my finger on."

Another friend commented, "My son is now five months old, and I've been through a really difficult period. I'm now being treated for postpartum depression, but the difficulty of being alone in the house with a baby for weeks/months is real. Especially for women who are used to being so active and having lots of independence and don't like asking for help. Even though I have tons of friends with babies and kids, I still feel isolated. In addition, new parents who are having a positive experience shout it from the rooftops—social media posts with hashtags like #iminlovewithmybaby are all over the place. This makes it easier to feel ashamed and very alone when not enjoying time with your baby as a new parent."

At the time, Adele's older child was three, and she had a four-month-old baby. Adele is a supervising attorney at one of the largest social justice organizations in New York City, where she has been an attorney for more than six years, providing legal services to NYC residents who need them most. In addition to spending so much time and energy on such a meaningful and impactful career, Adele told me how hard it was not to have time to herself as a new parent, because there was always another human who needed something from her.

This made it very difficult to have time to invest in friendships, especially with friends who don't have kids. It also was challenging to have time for her partner. Adele and her husband decided to exchange their weekly date night for self-time because they felt it was so important that each of them got their own time to be alone, exercise, go out for a pedicure, or have a drink with a friend. Without that self-time, working on their marriage wouldn't have even been possible.

In talking to Adele, I realized that most of us don't know how best to support our friends who are new parents and that we could all do a better job of being there for our friends taking care of little humans. I asked Adele (and a few of her fellow moms in a New Mothers Facebook Group she's a member of) if they had any thoughts on how we can show up more for our mom and dad friends. Here's a summary of what they had to say:

**1. If you don't have kids, don't assume that a new parent only wants to do baby things.** A lot of new moms express that having a baby makes them miss their old self and their old routines with friends. If you stop reaching out to your friend who recently had a baby, that can be very isolating for new moms. One woman wrote, "It's been important to find friends who feed different aspects of my life, instead of looking for one 'best friend' type who can be my ride or die. I've got childless friends who are creative types who I go see to talk shop and career friends who are great for developing myself (and vice versa!) professionally. Most of my very good pre-mom friends who don't have children, or don't plan on having children, are still important to me to maintain my whole self as 'not just a mom,' and I find it a breath of fresh air so that I don't have to talk about poop. But having my mom friends to talk to about poop is *just* as important."

**2. Make it as easy as possible for your mom friend.** Moms, especially working moms, have their hands full. Avoid adding stress or commitments to your mom friend's calendar. Go out of your way to make dinners and drop them off, offer to come over whenever is convenient (and understand if your mom friend has to cancel or reschedule), join for walking the baby or making a trip to the grocery store—just make yourself as supportive as possible and avoid adding any burdens to their lives.

My friend Sarah Peck, founder and executive director of Startup Pregnant, and a coach for mom entrepreneurs, told me: "One of the kindest things my nonparent friends have done for me is show up regularly to bring food, take us on day hikes, and plan adventures that the kids can join on. Sean, a twenty-seven-year-old when my first kid was born, came to our house on the weekends and cooked giant batches of chili and put large Tupperware containers into our freezer. It feels impossible at times to explain how hard parenting is—it's like running a marathon every day while having to do your job at the same time as running, and never getting to take a proper shower. Having friends who understand can feel so generous."

**3. Be flexible when making plans and communicating.** Sarah also recommends picking the right communications channel. "I have a few friends I text regularly, even though we barely see each other in person anymore," she says. "I text updates every week and send photos. I ask them questions about their lives. There are other friends I call when I'm on the spin bike and working out and a few friends I regularly catch up with on Voxer. Having those asynchronous, virtual channels to stay plugged in to their lives, even if we can't organize seeing each other in person as much for a while, has been a lift and a light."

**4. Create a support system.** Adele told me that the Baby Boomer mentality around parenting was "Toughen up; you'll figure it out!" Many millennial parents have trouble talking to their Boomer parents about this issue since a lot of Boomer parents will say, "Hey, we figured it out—and we didn't have YouTube videos on how to change a diaper or paid maternity leave—you'll figure it out, too." A more meaningful approach is to go out of your way to create a support network for your mom-friends and dad-friends who have young children. Perhaps you can create a meal train after your friend gives birth, show up to help with the baby as much as possible, or help mamas find resources when it comes to postpartum life, including books, podcasts, and postpartum-focused communities and meet-up groups.

# CREATE SAFE AND
# SUPPORTIVE SPACES

———

In 2015, a writer, speaker, and entrepreneur friend of mine named LC Johnson moved to Columbus, Ohio, with her husband. She didn't know anyone there except her husband and his family. Very soon after moving, LC felt a strong urge to connect with other women of color. LC, who is Black, felt like she had a lot of white women in her life and that finding white female friends wasn't a problem for her at work, coffee shops, and entrepreneurial events, but it was a lot harder to meet other women of color.

After having a dream about a space where Lauryn Hill was playing in the background and other women of color were working and hanging out together, LC knew she wanted to make that place a reality. Later that year, after she launched an Indiegogo crowdfunding campaign to raise start-up capital and get her first paying members, LC established Zora's House, a space where women of color could come to work, play, and socialize.

"I really thought we were going to be a coworking space with a focus on women of color," LC recalls. "But it became very clear that the word *coworking* was not resonating at all. It comes off as very white, very bro-y, very tech-y. In short, people's experiences with coworking weren't great.

At first, we thought we were in the business of selling space (with community as an add-on), but what we were really offering was community (with space as an add-on). Our purpose was bringing people together."

The name was inspired by Zora Neale Hurston, one of the most prolific Black authors during the Harlem Renaissance. LC loved that Zora wrote about women who cursed, smoked, and got divorced—with the message "You are powerful as you are." Although Zora was a highly acclaimed writer, the largest royalty she ever earned from her books was $943.75, and she died penniless in an unmarked grave in Florida in 1960. In 1973, author Alice Walker discovered and marked her grave and published "In Search of Zora Neale Hurston" in *Ms.*, which led to her revival. LC loves the story of how Alice Walker single-handedly brought Zora Neale Hurston's career back into the culture, "one woman of color bringing another into the light," exemplary of what Zora's House is all about.

Several years later, Zora's House is a nonprofit organization with seventy-five paying members and more than four hundred community members and has served as an inclusive learning space for the larger Columbus community to connect on issues of race, politics, economics, arts, and culture, relating to the identities and experiences of women of color. No one is turned away from Zora's House because they can't afford it, and the paying members help make this possible. Members must opt in to shared values like no racism, no sexism, no transphobia, and no homophobia.

Zora's House strives to embody Shine Theory, "a practice of mutual investment in each other . . . in helping someone be their best self—and relying on their help in return," developed by Aminatou Sow and Ann Friedman, who are best friends and cohosts of the popular *Call Your Girlfriend* podcast.

I share LC's belief that creating safe spaces for people to congregate, learn, and empower each other is revolutionary, especially for communities that have been consistently marginalized or underrepresented in positions of power and leadership. LC's work has not been without critics. Some white people in the community have asked why the space isn't open to everyone and even called it "reverse racism." They question why safe spaces like Zora's House are necessary. To these critics, LC will ask, "When's the last time you were the only white person in a room?" LC will remind them of the three Black men who had the police called on them simply for hanging out in a Starbucks. She'll explain why identity and shared experience matter, and matter the most for people who are not used to seeing their identities represented in public spaces.

Zora's House makes sure women of color see themselves in every aspect of the space. All the art on the walls is by women of color, the books on the shelves are by women of color authors, products available are sourced from women of color. Programming and events are designed to connect, empower, and elevate women of color, ranging from professional topics, like how to build a website in a day (taught by a woman of color); a doula training for women of color; a women of color–owned holiday market featuring work by women of color artisans in the community; and a watch party for Beyoncé's *Homecoming* documentary on Netflix, alongside a talk from a Ohio State University professor on Black women in the music industry.

Having women of color–centered programming allows the group to focus on issues of immediate concern to women of color. In the case of the doula training, the session focused on the experiences of Black women, who face higher maternal and infant mortality rates than other women (Black women are three to four times as likely to die from pregnancy-related causes as white women) and face unequal treatment in the quality of medical care they receive in this country. As LC puts it, "Sometimes we're just gonna be extra Black and be unapologetic about it."

By centering the experiences of Black women and other women of color, spaces like Zora's House allow for rich conversation and a sense of psychological safety that you just can't get in a space open to everyone. White people are welcome to attend events, but as a guest, to experience what it's like *not* to be centered in a space. People have traveled from as far away as California to visit Zora's House; and folks from Detroit, Chicago, and Atlanta have reached out to LC, curious about starting their own Zora's House in their city, showing just how vast the need is for more safe spaces like it.

When the pandemic hit, Zora's House shifted much of their programming online and made a twelve thousand dollar investment in technology to make their online platform more robust. They hosted virtual Sunday morning yoga featuring women of color yogis teaching yoga for women of color. After the police killings of George Floyd and Breonna Taylor, as the country protested systemic racism and police brutality against Black and brown people, Zora's House organized virtual healing circles for women of color to come together. LC told me these virtual gatherings were as powerful as anything that ever happened within the physical space, which made her realize that Zora's House wasn't just a physical house, it was a community without walls.

LC, who is raising two children *and* working a full-time job, all while running Zora's House, was reminded by one of her advisers that Black and brown people gathering has always been revolutionary in this country and that there is something very subversive, powerful, beautiful, and essential about creating and sustaining these types of spaces in our world.

# BRIDGE THE DIVIDE

One poll found that 7 percent of voters lost or ended a friendship because of the 2016 election and that many people chose not to be friends with people across the political divide. Political polarization is so intense that 80 percent of Americans now have "just a few" or *no friends* at all across the political aisle, according to Pew Research Center. In 2019, my friend Scott Keoni Shigeoka, a storyteller and Bridging Differences fellow for UC Berkeley's Greater Good Science Center, embarked on a journey to meet people with different perspectives and beliefs. He went on a road trip to rural Appalachia, attended Trump rallies in the Midwest, and visited evangelical Christian churches. Now he's writing a book about how to heal our country's divides and the importance of leveraging an underutilized resource: our curiosity.

A key guiding principle of Scott's work is recognizing there is individuality within groups. Growing up, Scott didn't want to be friends with anyone who was religious. He conflated religion with Christianity, and, as a queer person, he felt as though Christianity didn't see him or have space for him. As he's become older, he's realized there are more religions than Christianity and that not all Christians are the same. He's found churches across the country that have queer clergy and people within religious sects who are fighting for the rights of queer people. He stopped thinking of Christian or religious people as a monolith and started asking himself, *How do I become friends with more people who are religious?*

Attending Trump rallies in Minnesota showed Scott that people put on multiple versions of themselves. When he was outside of a rally, he had pretty respectful conversations with Trump supporters. He told them he was queer and progressive, and many people were impressed that he came to check out the rally and were welcoming and friendly. He met smart people with master's degrees who had interesting things to say, and he actually felt like there were people at the rally he could have been friends with. However, once they went inside and Donald Trump started talking, some things changed. It felt like the groupthink mentality took over and Trump was "othering" Scott and others out of the arena, and he no longer felt welcome or like he wanted to build a relationship with the people there.

Scott and his colleague, Jason Marsh, write that there's a difference between *agreement* and *understanding*. The goal of bridging differences is not to convince the other person of your viewpoint or even to build consensus. "Instead, the heart of bridging work lies in trying to understand someone else's perspective. While you might not share their views, you don't dismiss them; you dig deeper to try to appreciate where those views came from. This often requires asking questions and being willing to suspend judgment."

Kyla Sokoll-Ward, host of the podcast *Conversations That Don't Suck*, says that people are most fulfilled in conversations where they learn something about others *and themselves* at the same time. It's when they practice what Stephen R. Covey, author of *The 7 Habits of Highly Effective People*, called empathic listening: *listening to understand,* not just to respond. When they can turn their judgments into curiosities and try to find a part of themselves in another person, this helps create the bridge Scott is talking about.

It reminds me of the story of how Derek Black, the son of a grand wizard of the Ku Klux Klan, was once on a path to becoming the next leader of the white nationalist movement until he began questioning his worldview. Growing up, Derek had been homeschooled, but at the New College of Florida, he was exposed to people who didn't share his views, including several Jewish students who began inviting him to weekly Shabbat dinners. Gradually, Derek changed his views and eventually wrote an article in 2013, at the age of twenty-two, renouncing white nationalism.

It's important to note that Derek's transformation didn't happen overnight. It took many Shabbat dinners and efforts by his friends and fellow students to have difficult conversations with him.

Bridge-building takes time. It's also messy and complex work. Intrapersonal practices (like therapy, mindfulness, and compassionate listening) have helped Scott practice coping mechanisms and strategies to approach his relationships with more clarity and empathy. He admits that he doesn't always get it right and that bridging the divide requires both self-forgiveness and compassion toward others who are trying.

Scott's work proves that a real friendship is about risk. A real friendship is about being open to the views of other people. "The greatest risk in a friendship is that you and I will be transformed by other people," he says.

# BUILD AN
# EXPONENTIAL COMMUNITY

I call communities that have shaped my life *exponential communities* because they have a compounding impact on their members' potential, and I suggest you find one or two to join. In their seminal report about the future of community building, called "How We Gather," Angie Thurston and Casper ter Kuile, spiritual innovation researchers at Harvard Divinity School, argue that a new form of community—one that offers personal and social transformation—has become the new millennial religion. "Millennials are decidedly looking for spirituality and community in combination and feel they can't lead a meaningful life without it," they conclude.

An exponential community has your back, makes sure you're following your personal and professional dreams, and holds you accountable to your goals. Its members look at your goals and say, *I think you can do better.* The first time I learned about accountability was at the StartingBloc Institute for Social Innovation, a five-day leadership development program for young people interested in social change. Usually, when you go to a networking event and tell someone you're going to do something, they say, "Wow, that's wonderful, good for you," and they run off to get another beer. Not at StartingBloc, which has trained more than three thousand Fellows all over the world.

At StartingBloc, when I told my friend Evan that I wanted to quit my job to find more meaningful work, he called me every single week thereafter to ask if I had had "the talk" with my boss. Because Evan held me accountable, I finally did quit my job and began to pursue a path that was in alignment with my purpose. That led to a job where I was able to inspire *others* to reach their potential. Those people have gone on to launch new companies and get new jobs at innovative organizations. *Their* work is now touching the lives of countless people I'll never even meet.... And that's all in large part because of a supportive community that held me accountable to my dreams.

Moreover, exponential communities don't shy away from facilitating difficult conversations about building a more just and equitable society. StartingBloc Fellows like to put each other on the spot and ask, "How will this initiative help people of color or those with less privilege and access?" They take Brené Brown's words to heart when she says, "He or she who chooses comfort over courage and facilitating real conversations in towns and cities and synagogues and areas who need it; when you choose your own comfort over trying to bring people together, and you're a leader, either a civic leader or a faith leader, your days of relevance are numbered."

One of the greatest gifts that StartingBloc has given its Fellows is exposure to a diverse group of individuals. StartingBloc Fellows come from more than fifty-five countries and a variety of racial, ethnic, and religious backgrounds. Sixty-five percent of StartingBloc Fellows are people of color. Having friends who have different perspectives and life experiences than you matters. We can't separate the racism and xenophobia endemic to America from the fact that three-quarters of white Americans don't have any nonwhite friends. Without interracial friendships, it's pretty hard to dismantle white supremacy. It's imperative that all of us—especially white people—do the lifelong work to ensure the spaces and communities we're a part of are open and inclusive so they can truly be exponential.

If you've ever experienced being part of an exponential community, you've felt a magic that can't quite be described in words. It's a deep sensation that you are part of a family. That you are exactly where you need to be, that you are *home*. While studying religious groups in the early twentieth century, French sociologist Émile Dirkheim called this experience "collective effervescence," feeling like you're one with others, that you're moving in sync with a crowd. I felt this magic at StartingBloc, when I announced my intention to leave my job in 2012 in front of ninety-eight people I had never met before and received a standing ovation that carried me on a journey that eventually led to writing this book eight years later.

If I had to choose one word that comes close to describing this magical sensation, it would be *joy*. Exponential communities are made of joy and exist to make the world more joyous for others. The people you meet at networking events talk about their career accomplishments, and the people you meet at a bar talk about Instagram. In contrast, exponential communities talk about believing in the beauty of your dreams.

If you're having trouble finding a community like this near you, I've listed many in the online Resources Guide at smileyposwolsky. com/friendship.

# LIVE IN COMMUNITY

In 2019, I moved into a twelve-person co-living house in Oakland, California, and it changed my life for the better. Instead of checking social media first thing in the morning, I wake up every day excited to talk to two or three people I know I like in real life. I spend less time scrolling and more time cooking dinner with my roommates.

What I love most about my house, which we call "the Manor," is that the spaces in between being alone are filled with deep moments of connection. Living in community, at least when done right, means your home is invested in the growth and well-being of its housemates, and I really feel that at the Manor. Its residents care about the people they are living with. I've obviously felt that with my roommates in previous homes, but it's deeper and more intentional when you're living with twelve other people. It's less robotic ("How was your day?") and more powerful ("How was that difficult conversation with your boss about asking for more money?").

Moving into a community is like a warm blanket covering parts of your body that you didn't even know were freezing. When I go downstairs to the kitchen in the morning, someone is making coffee and we talk for a few minutes about how their date went last night. Actually,

I don't even need to go downstairs. I live on a floor with four of my dear friends, and we get to have stairwell conversations about our dating lives. We talked about creating a TV show called *Sex in the Town*.

When I'm making breakfast and someone else is also making breakfast, it turns into a five-person impromptu 11 a.m. brunch of pancakes, scrambled eggs, and bacon. At one house dinner, we did an exercise facilitated by one of my housemates where we each shared personal things about our childhoods, which brought us all a little closer together.

One Saturday night before I went out, I was having a snack with a friend, and then my housemate's friend came over, and my other housemate's friend showed up. The conversation went from inequalities in public speaking to working in refugee camps to how VR is being used for transformative psychedelic experiences.

People always just seem to "show up" at the Manor, like they just arrived out of thin air and appeared in the kitchen to have a snack, but they are always lovely, interesting people and the conversations we have always leave me thinking more deeply.

During COVID, we weren't allowing guests at the Manor (with twelve people, we were already a high-vector risk), and we had many hours-long meetings well into the night about how to keep each other safe. We developed strict cleaning protocols for cleaning the kitchen, sanitizing common areas, removing shoes at the front door, wearing masks outside of the house, and getting tested frequently. We had to get house approval before seeing someone outside our bubble and quarantine for two weeks (or get a negative COVID test) before reentering the house. When one of my housemates found out (from an Instagram pic) that our housemate had failed to tell our roommates ahead of time that he had gone on a camping trip with two friends, it turned into a tense house meeting about whether that housemate understood that living in a community meant doing what was safe for others, not just what felt safe for yourself.

Needless to say, living in a group house during a pandemic wasn't easy and required a lot of hard conversations and transparent communication. On the other hand, we definitely had more fun than most people during quarantine. With twelve people, you already have a sweet crew for a Sunday brunch, a dance party, board games, a poetry reading, a camping trip, a home workout class, gardening in the backyard, and bread baking and sauerkraut-making lessons, all of which my housemates participated in. We even hosted "TEDx Euclid," a social undistancing conference held on our patio (for ourselves, no outside guests—except my housemate's mom), and every housemate gave a five-minute presentation about something they cared about. My roomies talked about birding, Mumia Abu-Jamal, sourdough, mycelium, philosophy, and typography. I gave a short pitch for why friendship matters and ended with blasting "Hang with Me" by Robyn for a dancing time-out.

Usually, with everyone's busy work and travel schedules, very few of us are actually home at the same time, but during COVID, we were all working from home. A different person cooked dinner for the house every single night. In a time when most people were getting tired of sheltering in place alone or getting bored with spending every single night with their partner or their one roommate, we got to have a dinner party every single night. It felt almost like a speakeasy or a subversive activity since we were gathering with more than ten people—more than the local legal limit, but all of whom were part of our household. It was a huge benefit during the pandemic to be around friends and have that social contact so many of us were missing.

I don't expect you to live with twelve people (although check out co-living communities if you are interested), but I do encourage you to consider living with, or living near, people you care about. Just because so many adults live alone or with their partner doesn't mean you have to. There's a growing movement of people who realize that the benefits of co-living and multifamily cohousing are ever more important in the digital age. Wouldn't it be awesome to one day pool resources with your best friends and share a backyard, a beautiful garden, fresh vegetables, shopping duties, exercise equipment, tools, toys, child care, and weekly meals together—all while having your own kitchen, bathroom, and family space?!

You might even follow in the footsteps of four couples who've been best friends for twenty years and wanted to find a way to live closer together. They pooled their money and decided to build a settlement, called the "Llano Exit Strategy" (aka "Bestie Row"), made up of four tiny houses on the Llano River outside of Austin, Texas. The tiny homes are eco-friendly, sustainable, and only cost forty thousand dollars each. The four couples stay there as often as possible, taking a break from the hustle and bustle of Austin to be with each other and reconnect with nature. One day, they plan to retire together on the property.

# REMEMBER TO LET
# THE LIGHT IN

Chanukah, the Jewish festival of lights, has always been my favorite holiday. Not because of the eight nights of presents—although getting little "ha-ha's," as my mom calls them, is always fun—but because of the food. I love latkes. I remember thinking as a kid, "Wait, *we get to . . . we are supposed to . . . we have to* eat these delicious fried potato pancakes with applesauce?! This is unbelievable! I love being Jewish!" Every year I host a huge Chanukah party with my friends Ilana and Andrew. I put on an apron, chop onions for an hour, shred twenty pounds of potatoes, and fry latkes for one hundred people—it's my favorite day of the year.

In December 2016, I spent the eight days of Chanukah with Levi and his family in Pismo, California. Levi was in the final stages of his year-long battle with brain cancer. He had already lost mobility on the right side of his body, and two of us had to help him stand up and carry him to the bathroom. Despite his frailty, Levi would make jokes as he limped his way to the toilet. When his brother Seth farted, he would say, his voice barely audible, "That sounds good." When I asked him if he could hear me, he'd respond, "What did you say, Smiley?" When Levi's partner, Brooke, asked him what he was thinking about, he answered,

"The Earth." One day, we went out for tacos and Levi poured some of his Pacifico into the salsa just to see if anyone would eat it.

For Chanukah, I gave Levi a photo book full of memories from college, Burning Man, and Camp Grounded. When he was looking through these photos, his face was sometimes deadpan and I worried that he wasn't able to recognize his best friends; but every minute or so, he'd manage a half-smile and let out a little cackle.

Levi's mom, Bluma, and I made latkes in the kitchen, and Levi must have eaten eleven of them, smothering each with sour cream and apple-sauce. After dinner, Levi would make silly faces at me until I snuck him an extra piece of Oreo cheesecake.

He was messing with us until the very end.

The next day, I said goodbye to Levi for the last time. I'm pretty sure he whispered the words "I love you, too" when I told him I loved him forever, but he may well have said, "Get out of here, Smiley, so I can pass out and have enough energy tomorrow to watch season 4 of *Game of Thrones*," I'm just not sure.

That week, I remember video chatting with groups of friends who were spending their holidays together. So many of these friends had met because of Camp Grounded and Levi's work. Levi was not in those video chats (he was not in Oakland, San Francisco, LA, or New York) but he was *there* because there would be no *there* without him. Every time I hear someone say one of our camp mantras—"You're awesome!" and "If you can hear me, clap twice!" and "Shut up and be grateful" and "F*ck you, inner critic!" and "Be vulnerageous" and "One new friend, one new friend!"—I think of Levi because, without him, those sayings wouldn't be part of our collective consciousness.

Levi passed away two weeks later, and that Chanukah in Pismo will stay with me for the rest of my life. As sad as those days were, I remember feeling like time was on hold. Like every moment we had together was a blessing. Like we were getting the miracle of a few more days with Levi, just like the Maccabees got from their tiny jar of oil many generations ago.

Within the first year after the passing of a loved one, it's traditional for Jewish families to gather for an unveiling ceremony to dedicate the gravestone. At Levi's unveiling, his brother Seth shared a note from one of Levi's doctors at the hospital, who had been inspired by how graciously Levi faced his cancer and the treatment. Levi stayed positive even though he was losing his hair, and he painted the other chemo patients' nails blue.

We placed little trinkets around Levi's gravestone: crystals, sea shells, rocks, buttons, tiny hands, and a Dark Chocolate Almond Mint KIND Bar wrapper. Brooke brought glitter blue nail polish, and we painted our nails just like Levi had done for his fellow cancer patients. Brooke shared that Levi always said that you could never be mad at someone who was wearing glitter nail polish and that it was hard to be mean if you were wearing glitter nail polish. We gathered around the gravesite, cried, and then laughed when we concluded that Levi demanded us to move the headstone five inches to the left to be in the shade of a nearby tree.

After the unveiling, we ate pizza, told stories, and listened to a song by Levi's high school punk band. We sang "The Weight" by the Band and "Mykonos" by Fleet Foxes. Seth even sang "It Wasn't Me" by Shaggy. Then we all piled into the living room to watch the blue-orange-purple sunset. I could hear Levi's mischievous voice in my ear saying, "Magic hour, maaaaaagic hour!"

With all the darkness in the world, Levi taught me that it's moments like these—moments when time disappears, when you forget to look at your phone, when you forget you even have a phone—that are the opposite of loneliness and at the heart of any life worth living. This was Levi's light—slowing down time, extending and expanding these moments, making them more intentional, heartfelt, playful, and beautiful.

# *You Have to Decide What Kind of Friend You Want to Be*

It was October 2015 in Austin, Texas, and our last Camp Grounded for the season had just ended. It was hot—110 degrees in Texas in late October hot. We were exhausted.

I was laid out on the grass in the shade with Levi, who was looking through his cardboard inbox, showing me all the thank-you notes campers had handwritten him over the weekend. There were probably seventy-five notes in his inbox. One was from a camper who said that three weeks before camp, he had thought about taking his own life, but camp made him decide he was going to keep going. Another was from a camper who said that, for the first time in his life, he felt comfortable as a gay man around straight men. Another was from a camper who said camp was the single most powerful experience of her life and that she finally felt ready to quit the job she hated to spend her life doing something she cared about.

There were countless notes like these, and Levi read every single one. That was the last camp he ever went to—he was diagnosed with brain cancer just a few months later—and I'll always remember him reading those notes of gratitude.

I would like to close this book by sharing something Levi wrote on his thirty-second birthday, just six months before he passed away. Levi posted this on his Facebook wall, and I'm sure he is somewhere right now, eating sushi and listening to "The Weight" by the Band, giving me shit for quoting something he wrote on Facebook in my book all about in-person connection. Oh, the irony! I'm sorry, buddy; I'll send you some sushi. Here's what Levi shared:

I'M ALIVE, PUSHING FORWARD AND DOING WELL!!

32 years ago, TODAY, I was BORN. As of right now, I have never felt MORE ALIVE.

I would be lying if I said that the last 5 months have been easy. However, with all your support and love, I continue pushing forward with a smile. I often even forget that I have Cancer—that's my favorite part of it all. (There it is, the "C" word). Truly though, in moments when I might start to feel down, I find myself with people who lift me up, make me laugh and give me a body to squeeze—or they wrap their arms around me when I'm being stubborn, take me to the beach, and we put sand dollars on our eyes. It's pretty amazing to have such close friends, a tight family and a wide community that shows so much love! I don't know what I'd do without each one of you!! . . .

There is so much more I'd like to share. So much . . .

But more than anything, I want you to close your eyes and take that deep breath you remember from childhood. Think about those who are, were, and have been closest to you. Open your eyes and call that family member, that long-lost friend, that person who you've lost touch with, a sibling you've been meaning to call. This is my gift back to you, as we are all a gift to each other. Day by day, breath by breath, enjoy each and every moment you have. This moment is all we got and that is awesome!

Happy Birthday to All Of Us!

So much love.
#WeGotThis

—Levi aka Fidget

Above all else, Levi taught me that you don't have to live life the way the world tells you to.

You can create the world you want to live in.

You can question what it means to be a grown-up.

You can make one new friend anytime you go anywhere.

You can hug more and hug longer.

You can make gratitude, not checking Insta, your evening ritual.

You can become a Correspondence Queen.

You can be a Sheriff of Good Times.

You can be less flaky.

You can sneak a card into your friend's bag when they leave your house.

You can eat dinner with your friends across the country on Zoom—even if there's not a pandemic.

You can listen to a full Radiohead album with someone you love.

You can be a man who isn't afraid to get vulnerable and emotional around other men in your life.

You can knock on the door of an older neighbor and see if they want someone to talk to.

You can celebrate the simple yet revolutionary act of getting your dopamine from spending more time with your friends.

You can be a Minister for Loneliness in your community.

You can make human connection the true currency of life.

Remember: you have to decide what kind of friend you want to be.

*Make human connection the true currency of life.*

# Spread the Love

...............

Friendship is contagious. If you found this book useful, please share it with your friends as a way of spreading the love and helping others find more connection. There are a number of easy ways to do this:

1. Gift this book to a friend or stranger who needs to read it.
2. Write an Amazon or Goodreads review of the book.
3. Post a selfie with the book on Instagram! #FriendshipOverLoneliness
4. Host a friendship-themed dinner party at your house (or virtually!). Discussion Questions are available at the link below.
5. Add your favorite friendship ritual to the Friendship Ritual Library (link below).
6. Check out my Resources Guide. Discover books, podcasts, communities, and experiences that can help you meet like-minded people, make new friends, and build your community.

Discussion Questions, Ritual Library, and Resources Guide:
**smileyposwolsky.com/friendship**

### CRISIS TEXT LINE

If you are in a crisis or feel like you need to talk to someone, please know there are people out there for you. Crisis Text Line can help you or a friend deal with loneliness. Reach a counselor by texting HOME to 741741 for free 24/7 support, or visit crisistextline.org.

# Acknowledgments

I want to start by expressing gratitude and love for the Camp Grounded community: this book is because of you. Thank you for showing me what friendship in the digital age feels like.

This book would not have been possible without my friends who shared their stories and friendship rituals with me. I'm grateful for everyone who gave their time to be interviewed, and for my colleagues who create human connection every day: Alanna Mednick, Alexis Scott, Amber Rae, Andrew Horn, Ankit Shah, Ashanti Branch, Bailey Robinson, Brady Gill, Brent Schulkin, Chelsea Coleman, Dr. Emily Anhalt, Evan Kleiman, Christine Lai, Casper ter Kuile, Catherine Woodiwiss, Dev Aujla, Gayle Abrams, Hayli Rutledge, Hunter Franks, Ilana Lipsett, Ivan Cash, Jeanine Cerendolo, Jenny Sauer-Klein, Jillian Richardson, Joanna Miller, Josh Kelley, Kasley Killam, Kat Vellos, Kyla Sokoll-Ward, Lauren Weinstein, LC Johnson, Liz Travis Allen, Logan Ury, Dr. Marisa G. Franco, Michael Liskin, Molly Sonseng, Ned Buskirk, Paloma Herman, Raman Frey, Sahar Massachi, Sara Weinberg, Scott Shigeoka, Shasta Nelson, Ted and Franziska Gonder, and Vika Viktoria.

My people are people who bring people together. Thank you to everyone out there working hard to foster friendship and connection in the age of loneliness. Special thanks to those who inspired me from afar while I was writing this book: Priya Parker, Johann Hari, Sherry Turkle, Tristan Harris and the Center for Humane Technology, Max Stossel, Cal Newport, Brené Brown, Krista Tippett, Maria Popova, Rebecca Solnit, Jia Tolentino, Ann Friedman, Aminatou Sow, Lydia Denworth, Jenny Odell, Dan Schawbel, Radha Agrawal, Vivek Murthy, Stacey Abrams, and AOC.

To my wonderful agent, Lindsay Edgecombe, and the entire team at Levine Greenberg Rostan: thank you for believing in this project from the beginning, and thank you for always going to bat for me. Danielle Svetcov and Rebecca Rodd: thank you for guiding the final stretch. Dominic Yarabe: thank you for your early feedback and support on my book proposal.

Thank you to my talented editor Jess Riordan for making the manuscript better and being my champion at Running Press. To the entire Running Press/Hachette team: thank you for bringing this project to life. Special thanks to: Joanna Price, Amanda Richmond, Kristin Kiser, Jessica Schmidt, Alina O'Donnell, Kara Thornton, and Amy Cianfrone.

Thank you to Samantha Russo for your beautiful cover design, Adam Greenberg for early edits and feedback on my proposal, and Asya Azar for taking photos of me.

Thank you to everyone who has supported my work in recent years. Special thanks to: SpeakInc (Rich Gibbons, Jeff Bigelow, Tim Mathy, Lisa Coleman, Nicole DeMers, Erin Lapeyre); Washington Speakers Bureau (Allyson Musci, Kevin Jeske); BigSpeak (Barrett Cordero, Kyle Munger); Rhonda Payne, Karen Bernstein, and everyone at ASAE; CAMPUSPEAK (David Stollman and Luke Davis); Hung Pham and Culture Summit; The Culture Conference; Duleesha Kulasooriya and Deloitte; Robin Meyerhoff, Richard Green, and SAP; Ashley Wilson and MailChimp; Cheryl Fraenzl, Tanja Roos, and Esalen Institute; Markus von der Lühe and Year of the X; Jeremy Duhon, Jason Dilg, and TEDxMileHigh; Stacy Horne and The Battery; Sarah Shewey and EXP; Josh Linkner, Matt Ciccone, and 3 Ring Circus; Colette Crespin, Iris Yee, and Burning Man; Forest Bronzan and Digital Detox.

Thank you to the StartingBloc community for shaping who I am today, Hive for introducing me to so many good people, and Wesleyan University for introducing me to my best friends.

To the members and champions of The Women/Womxn, BIPOC, and Inclusivity Speaker Initiative: thank you to everyone who is working to increase representation and equity in public speaking and across all industries.

To my Author Group: thank you for getting me pumped about writing a book during the pandemic. I miss our Zoom dance parties!

To my roomies/homies at the Manor: thank you for giving me friendship in a time of loneliness; Zev Felix, Ilana Lipsett, Jay Standish, Evan Steiner, Anna Akullian, Melissa Wong, Simone Stolzoff, Navvab Tabjvar, Willie Jackson, Nathan Meyers, Dasha Gorlova, Martha Tesfalul, Brent Schulkin, Lindy Rauchenstein, April Harper, Kendall Warson, Neha Sharma, Tom and Ellie Llewellyn.

To my wonderful friends who give me joy and remind me what matters most, especially: Andreas Mendez-Peñate, Manuela Igel, Jesse Brenner, Gabe Prager, Kevin Haas, Margie Albarran, Zeb Zankel, Sarah Jesse, Phil Amidon, Bettina Schlegel, Daniel Kahn, Phil Sima, Zev Felix, Seth Felix, Brooke Dean, Ian Evans, Ilana Lipsett, Brady Gill, Sile Bao, Jenny Feinberg, Satya Kamdar, Kelly McFarling, Andrew Brennan, Andy Saxon, Dar Vanderbeck, Alex McPhillips, Brian Thomas, Conor Gleason, Jacob Hudson, Evan Walden, Christine Lai, Katrina Gordon, Emily Anhalt, Eve Peters, Jana Hirsch, Paloma Herman, Cassidy Blackwell, Morgan Davis, Natanya Biskar, Liz Beedy, EJ Winter, Ashley Hodge, Emma Sherwood-Forbes, Emily Dreyfuss, Seth Shipman, Emily Pfeiffer, Rachel Pecker, Elizabeth Langston, Noah Issacs, David Rood-Ojalvo, Diego Ortiz, Sara Covey, Grace Lesser, Andrew Casden, Booth Haley, Iris Yee, Ryan Goldberg, Scott Goldberg, Ashley Rose Hogrebe, Kelsey Freeman, Hana Nobel, Kelly Rogala, Jesse Rogala, Emma Toll, Katie Roche, Evan Kleiman, Adam Ward, Taylor Mee-Lee, Ben Madden, Joe Madden, Lyndsey Madden, Andrew Buresh, Karen Joe, Jordan Spiers, Kasey Luber, João Montenegro, Jonah Spear, Kiki Lipsett, Megan Lipsett, Alanna Mednick, Evan Gelfand, Terra Judge, Jay Standish, Justin Oliver, Jolene Anello, Allie Stark, Ben Hanna, Mandy Hixson, Nick Baker, Liz Allen, Sophie Speer, Josiah Johnson, Forest Stearns, Torie Beedle, Adam Rosendahl, Ivan Cash, Carla Fernandez, Ben Provan, Sarah Cabell, Mike Zuckerman, Josh Gelfand, Mordechai Weiner, Matthew Wetschler, Cam Adair, Nate Bagley, Ben Tseitlin, Amber Rae, Farhad Attaie, Andrew Horn, Vika Viktoria, Craig Forman, Jenny Sauer-Klein,

Lauren Burke, Julia Winston, Antonio Neves, Cosmo Fujiyama, Cesar Gonzalez, Matt Fitzgerald, Shira Abramowitz, Monica Kang, Sarah Waxman, Sarah Seegal, Alana Corbett, Palomi Sheth, Logan Ury, Samantha Stein, Bernadette Cay, Brian Weinberg, David Spinks, Minda Harts, Sarah Peck, Meredith Hubbel, Tristan Harris, Max Stossel, Jessica Semaan, Janet Frishberg, Claire Williams, Jayson Carpenter, Sumeet Banerji, Caroline Kessler, Bernat Fortet, Duleesha Kulasooriya, Adam Elmaghraby, Melissa Whippo, Paula Tranchida, Tigre Peyrú, Kwesi Roberts, Kyla O'Neill, Gayle Abrams, Meredith Pierce, Ann Garcia, Abraham Weiner, Nate Kauffman, Catherine Woodiwiss, Brian Segal, Kevin Fanfoni, Minh Nguyen, Lisa Lee, Matt Lock, Saya Iwasaki, Alex Dang, Annie Svigals, and Chris Chapman.

To Bluma and Edward Felix, Zev Felix, Seth Felix, and Brooke Dean: thank you for your light, thank you for everything.

To Ali: thank you for your love and support—this is our house, we make the rules—te quiero. To Fred Pflaum, Linda Demers, and Marjorie Pflaum: thank you for hosting me at the Lake during the pandemic, it was the perfect place to write this book. To Freda and the Wagner family: thank you for your ongoing support.

Most importantly, thank you to my family: Mom, Dad, Becca, Gemma, Luka, Remy, and Aunt Michelle: I love you more than the world. Thank you to everyone that continues to carry me on my journey. You know who you are. I love you and I am forever grateful.

# Notes

....................

Some excerpts in this book have been adapted from "The Man Who Gave Us All the Things," an obituary for Levi Felix that I wrote on Medium and earlier versions of writing I've shared on Medium and social media.

## PREFACE: THE POWER OF FRIENDSHIP IN A PANDEMIC

**Service Workers Coalition, raising more than eighty thousand dollars.** Ryan Sutton, "How NYC Restaurant Workers Are Getting Help So Far," *Eater New York*, March 19, 2020. https://ny.eater.com/2020/3/13/21179235/labor-sick-leave-coronavirus-testing-nyc-restaurants

**Minnesota COVIDSitters, with their tagline.** Jia Tolentino, "What Mutual Aid Can Do During a Pandemic," *The New Yorker*, May 11, 2020. https://www.newyorker.com/magazine/2020/05/18/what-mutual-aid-can-do-during-a-pandemic

**observed Kat Vellos, friendship expert and author of *We Should Get Together*.** Dr. Ely Weinschneider, "'Being forced into isolation has made it abundantly clear how much we mean to other, and how much we need each other.' With Kat Vellos," *Thrive Global*, March 29, 2020. https://thriveglobal.com/stories/being-forced-into-isolation-has-made-it-abundantly-clear-how-much-we-mean-to-each-other-and-how-much-we-need-each-other-with-kat-vellos

**In Bernal Heights, my partner's neighborhood.** Nellie Bowles, "In Lockdown, a Neighborhood Opens Up," *New York Times*, May 30, 2020. https://www.nytimes.com/2020/05/30/technology/bernal-heights.html

**Sherry Turkle, Abby Rockefeller Mauzé Professor of the Social Studies of Science and Technology at MIT wrote.** Sherry Turkle, Quoted in "Coronavirus Will Change the World Permanently. Here's How," *Politico Magazine*, March 19, 2020. https://www.politico.com/news/magazine/2020/03/19/coronavirus-effect-economy-life-society-analysis-covid-135579

**study published in the journal *American Psychologist*.** Alison Escalante MD, "We Are Not Lonely During Social Distancing After All," *Psychology Today*, July 6, 2020. https://www.psychologytoday.com/us/blog/shouldstorm/202007/we-are-not-lonely-during-social-distancing-after-all

## INTRODUCTION: THE REVOLUTIONARY ACT OF CONNECTION IN THE DIGITAL AGE

***State of Friendship in America* report, the social research organization Lifeboat found.** Lifeboat, "State of Friendship in America Report: A Crisis of Confidence," May 21, 2013. https://static1.squarespace.com/static/5560cec6e4b0cc18bc63ed3c/t/55625cabe4b0077f-89b718ec/1432509611410/lifeboat-report.pdf

**average American hasn't made a new friend in the last five years.** Ben Renner, "Survey: Average American Hasn't Made a New Friend—In 5 Years!, Study Finds," October 19, 2019. Survey commissioned by Evite, conducted by OnePoll. https://www.studyfinds.org/survey-average-american-hasnt-made-new-friend-in-5-years

**BBC reported that 200,000 people haven't spoken to a close relative.**
"Two thirds of UK adults have 'nobody to talk to' about problems," *BBC News*, February 1, 2018. https://www.bbc.com/news/health-42903914

**55,000-person BBC survey.** Claudia Hammond, "Who feels lonely? The results of the world's largest loneliness study," *BBC Radio 4*, October 1, 2018. https://www.bbc.co.uk/programmes/articles/2yzhf-v4DvqVp5nZyxBD8G23/who-feels-lonely-the-results-of-the-world-s-largest-loneliness-study

**In a national Cigna survey of 10,000 US adults in 2019.** "Loneliness and the Workplace: 2020 U.S. Report," Cigna, January 23, 2020. https://www.cigna.com/static/www-cigna-com/docs/about-us/newsroom/studies-and-reports/combatting-loneliness/cigna-2020-loneliness-factsheet.pdf

**According to the Pew Research Center, 90 percent of eighteen- to twenty-nine-year-olds regularly use social media.** "Social Media Use in 2018," Pew Research Center, March 1, 2018. https://www.pewresearch.org/internet/2018/03/01/social-media-use-in-2018

**45 percent of teens.** "Teens, Social Media & Technology 2018," Pew Research Center, May 31, 2018. https://www.pewresearch.org/internet/2018/05/31/teens-social-media-technology-2018

**TikTok—the number one downloaded app of 2020.** Katie Sehl, "20 Important TikTok Stats Marketers Need to Know in 2020," Hootsuite Blog, May 7, 2020. https://blog.hootsuite.com/tiktok-stats

**has linked rising rates of teen mental health challenges . . . to smartphone and social media use.** Jean M. Twenge, "Have Smartphones Destroyed a Generation?," *The Atlantic*, September 2017. https://www.theatlantic.com/magazine/archive/2017/09/has-the-smartphone-destroyed-a-generation/534198

**suicide rate for young people aged ten to twenty-four increased by 56 percent.** Sally C. Curtin, MA, and Melonie Heron, PhD, "Death Rates Due to Suicide and Homicide Among Persons Aged 10–24: United States, 2000–2017," CDC: National Center for Health Statistics Data Brief No. 352, October 2019. https://www.cdc.gov/nchs/data/databriefs/db352-h.pdf

**Jane Brody . . . reminds us that people can be socially isolated and not feel lonely.** Jane Brody, "The Surprising Effects of Loneliness on Health," *New York Times*, December 11, 2017. https://www.nytimes.com/2017/12/11/well/mind/how-loneliness-affects-our-health.html

**psychologists Julianne Holt-Lunstad and Timothy B. Smith.** Julianne Holt-Lunstad and Timothy B. Smith, "Loneliness and social isolation as risk factors for CVD: implications for evidence-based patient care and scientific inquiry," *Heart* 102, no. 13 (July 2016). https://heart.bmj.com/content/heartjnl/102/13/987.full.pdf

**We tap our phones 2,600 times a day.** Julia Naftulin, "Here's how many times we touch our phones every day," *Business Insider*, July 13, 2016. https://www.businessinsider.com/dscout-research-people-touch-cell-phones-2617-times-a-day-2016-7#

**look at our phones every twelve minutes.** "Brits Now Check Their Mobile Phones Every 12 Minutes," *Huffington Post UK*, February 8, 2018. https://www.huffingtonpost.co.uk/entry/brits-now-check-their-mobile-phones-every-12-minutes_uk_5b62bf60e4b0b15aba9fe3cb

**50 minutes a day on Facebook.** James B. Stewart. "Facebook Has 50 Minutes of Your Time Each Day. It Wants More," *New York Times*, May 5, 2016. https://www.nytimes.com/2016/05/06/business/facebook-bends-the-rules-of-audience-engagement-to-its-advantage.html

**spend just 4 percent . . . of our time with friends.** Lifeboat, "State of Friendship in America Report: A Crisis of Confidence," May 21, 2013. https://static1.squarespace.com/static/5560cec6e4b0cc18bc63ed3c/t/ 55625cabe4b0077f89b718ec/1432509611410/lifeboat-report.pdf

**Johann . . . shares in his TED Talk.** Johann Hari, "Johann Hari: Everything you think you know about addiction is wrong," TED video, TEDGlobalLondon, June 2015. https://www.ted.com/talks/ johann_hari_everything_you_think_you_know_about_addiction_is_ wrong?language=en

**science journalist Lydia Denworth reveals.** Elena Renken, "Survival of the Friendliest: How Our Close Friendships Help Us Thrive," *NPR*, February 22, 2020. https://www.npr.org/sections/health-shots/2020/02/22/807742275/survival-of-the-friendliest-how-our-close-friendships-help-us-thrive

*healthy relationships* **are the key to a long and healthy life . . . says Robert Waldinger.** Robert Waldinger, "Robert Waldinger: What makes a good life? Lessons from the longest study on happiness," TED video, TEDxBeaconStreet, November 2015. https://www.ted. com/talks/robert_waldinger_what_makes_a_good_life_lessons_from_ the_longest_study_on_happiness?language=en

**Warren Buffett, one of the wealthiest and most powerful men in the world, agrees.** Jenny Anderson, "The only metric of success that really matters is the one we ignore," *Quartz*, March 12, 2019. https:// qz.com/1570179/how-to-make-friends-build-a-community-and-create-the-life-you-want

## PART ONE: BE MORE PLAYFUL

**I was a freshman at Wesleyan University in 2001 . . . We used land-lines.** I told a version of this story in a TEDx talk I gave in 2019. "Smiley Poswolsky: The unexpected cure for millennial burnout," TED Video, TEDxWesleyanU, August 23, 2019. https://www.youtube.com/watch?v=4b29Gd-Eb00

**He would often caution us, noting that 60 percent.** Statistics from digitaldetox.org. For more facts about the invisible harms of technology, check out the Center for Humane Technology's Ledger of Harms: https://ledger.humanetech.com

**Tristan Harris . . . "There's a hidden goal driving the direction of all the technology we make."** Tristan Harris, "Tristan Harris: How a handful of tech companies control billions of minds every day," TED Video, TED2017, April 2017. https://www.ted.com/talks/tristan_harris_how_a_handful_of_tech_companies_control_billions_of_minds_every_day. Learn more about the vital work Tristan is doing at the Center for Humane Technology: humanetech.com

**Priya Parker teaches us . . . "The amazing thing about gatherings is that, for a limited, temporary moment in time."** Motley Fool Staff, "Priya Parker on Gathering: Don't Be Chill'—You're Creating a Temporary World," Rule Breaker Investing Podcast with David Garner, August 17, 2018. https://www.fool.com/investing/2018/08/17/priya-parker-on-gathering-dont-be-chill-youre-crea.aspx

**Mandy Len Catron's popular "Modern Love" essay.** Mandy Len Catron, "To Fall in Love with Anyone, Do This," *New York Times*, January 9, 2015. https://www.nytimes.com/2015/01/11/style/modern-love-to-fall-in-love-with-anyone-do-this.html

**My favorite question is #33.** Daniel Jones, "The 36 Questions That Lead to Love," *New York Times*, January 9, 2015. https://www.nytimes.com/2015/01/09/style/no-37-big-wedding-or-small.html

**On their tenth date, Dev and Liz went on a ten-day trip across the North Atlantic.** Dev Aujla, "Relationships Move Fast on a Slow Cargo Ship," *New York Times*, April 3, 2020. https://www.nytimes.com/2020/04/03/style/modern-love-coronavirus-isolation-cargo-ship.html

**The oxytocin release that comes from hugging.** Harvard Medical School, "In brief: Hugs heartfelt in more ways than one," Harvard Health Publishing website, March 2014. https://www.health.harvard.edu/newsletter_article/In_brief_Hugs_heartfelt_in_more_ways_than_one

**Carnegie Mellon University found that people who received regular hugs had fewer flu symptoms.** Shilo Rea, "Hugs Help Protect Against Stress and Infection, Say Carnegie Mellon Researchers," Carnegie Mellon University website, December 17, 2014. https://www.cmu.edu/news/stories/archives/2014/december/december17_hugsprotect.html

**philosophy professor Stephen Asma writes.** Stephen T. Asma, "This Friendship Has Been Digitized," *New York Times*, March 23, 2019. https://www.nytimes.com/2019/03/23/opinion/this-friendship-has-been-digitized.html

**A study in the journal *Adolescence* that looked at forty-nine cultures.** Andrew Reiner, "The Power of Touch, Especially for Men," *New York Times*, December 5, 2017. https://www.nytimes.com/2017/12/05/well/family/gender-men-touch.html

**podcast interview with Radha Agrawal.** "Radha Agrawal: How to Build Community for Personal Happiness and Professional Impact," What's the Big Idea with Andrew Horn, Podcast, August 15, 2019.

**As the Burning Man website states.** Burning Man, "The 10 Principles of Burning Man," Burning Man website. https://burningman.org/culture/philosophical-center/10-principles

## PART TWO: BE A BETTER FRIEND

**In Brené Brown's book *Braving the Wilderness*.** Brené Brown, *Braving the Wilderness: The Quest for True Belonging and the Courage to Stand Alone* (New York: Random House, 2017).

**the mushroom farmer that Mr. Rogers had interviewed on the show.** In my book *The Quarter-Life Breakthrough*, I incorrectly remembered that I met Fred Rogers himself. My parents recently told me that it wasn't Mr. Rogers, it was the mushroom farmer!

**Fred Rogers . . . Senate Subcommittee on Communications in 1969.** Maxwell Strachan, "The Best Argument for Saving Public Media Was Made by Mr. Rogers in 1969," *Huffington Post*, March 16, 2017. https://www.huffpost.com/entry/mr-rogers-pbs-budget-cuts_n_58ca8d-6fe4b0be71dcf1d440

**Fred Rogers quoted Henry James saying.** "Three Things in Human Life Are Important. The First Is to Be Kind . . ." Quote Investigator website, September 21, 2018. https://quoteinvestigator.com/2018/09/21/kind

**"Here's what I mean by emotional fitness," [Dr. Anhalt] says.** "Hit the Emotional Gym—The Founder's Framework for Emotional Fitness," Interview with Dr. Emily Anhalt, PsyD, in *First Round Review*, 2020. https://firstround.com/review/hit-the-emotional-gym-the-founders-framework-for-emotional-fitness

**seven traits of emotional fitness.** Ibid.

"Starting a meditation habit . . ." Ibid.

**a third of Americans . . . showed signs of clinical anxiety or depression in May 2020.** Alyssa Fowers and William Wan, "A third of Americans now show signs of anxiety of depression, Census Bureau finds amid coronavirus pandemic," *Washington Post*, May 26, 2020. https://www.washingtonpost.com/health/2020/05/26/americans-with-depression-anxiety-pandemic/?arc404=true

**Dr. Anhalt's excellent emotional fitness tips: do a weekly relationship retrospective.** @dremilyanhalt. "Emotional fitness tip for couples & cofounders, Do a weekly relationship retro." *Twitter*, August 1, 2020.

**As Aristotle said, "Friendship is the art . . ."** Maria Popova, "Anam Cara and the Essence of True Friendship: Poet and Philosopher John O'Donohue on the Beautiful Ancient Celtic Notion of Soul-Friend," *Brain Pickings*, August 12, 2015. https://www.brainpickings.org/2015/08/12/anam-cara-john-o-donohue-soul-friend

**Kyla Sokoll-Ward, a loneliness expert and host of the podcast *Conversations That Don't Suck*.** Learn more about Kyla Sokoll-Ward's work: kylasw.com

**70 percent of millennials experience burnout and 30 percent.** Ryan Pendell, "Millennials Are Burning Out," *Gallup*, July 19, 2018. https://www.gallup.com/workplace/237377/millennials-burning.aspx

**According to Dan Schawbel, connection expert and author of *Back to Human*.** Tom Bilyeu, "Stop Looking at Your Phone—It's Killing You, Dan Schawbel on Impact Theory," YouTube Video, March 26, 2019. https://www.youtube.com/watch?v=hi7FOwnbYro

the best employees are those who have a best friend at work. Tom Rath and Jim Harter, "Your Friends and Your Social Well-Being," Gallup, August 19, 2020. https://news.gallup.com/businessjournal/127043/friends-social-wellbeing.aspx

In *The Business of Friendship,* **Shasta Nelson shows.** Shasta Nelson, *The Business of Friendship: Making the Most of Our Relationships Where We Spend Most of Our Time* (New York: HarperCollins Leadership, 2020).

## PART THREE: INVEST IN FRIENDSHIP

**research by Jeffery A. Hall . . . suggests that you need to spend at least ninety hours.** "How to Make Friends? Study Reveals Time It Takes," The University of Kansas News website, March 28, 2018. https://news.ku.edu/2018/03/06/study-reveals-number-hours-it-takes-make-friend

**psychologist and friendship expert Dr. Marisa Franco.** Learn more about Dr. Marisa Franco's work: drmarisafranco.com

**In one of her SuperSoul Sessions, Brené Brown offers the useful analogy.** Brené Brown, "SuperSoul Sessions: The Anatomy of Trust," Video on Brené Brown's website. https://brenebrown.com/videos/anatomy-trust-video

**In her book *Frientimacy,* Shasta [Nelson] shares.** Shasta Nelson, *Friedtimacy: How to Deepen Friendships for Lifelong Health and Happiness* (Berkeley, CA: Seal Press, 2016).

**Sherry Turkle's words in her book *Reclaiming Conversation.*** Sherry Turkle, *Reclaiming Conversation: The Power of Talk in the Digital Age* (New York: Penguin Press, 2015).

**As community building expert Casper ter Kuile says.** Gathering Summit, "Reimagining spirituality: Casper ter Kuile, coauthor of How We Gather," YouTube Video, February 23, 2020. https://www.youtube.com/watch?v=6yqbPcRw5gs&t=1s

**Lauren Weinstein recommends making a visual representation of your friends called a Friend Circle.** Lauren's Friend Circle was the first Friend Circle visual I've seen. However, in my research since, I discovered different versions of Friend Circle exercises. Another is included in Kate Leaver's book, *The Friendship Cure: Reconnecting in the Modern World* (New York: The Overlook Press, 2018).

**Lauren calls this circle Tier 1.** I've also seen various breakdowns of the different friendship tiers. A great one is included in a blog post by Tim Urban, "10 Types of Odd Friendships You're Probably Part Of," *Wait But Why*, December 8, 2014. https://waitbutwhy.com/2014/12/10-types-odd-friendships-youre-probably-part.html

**British anthropologist Robin Dunbar.** Robin Dunbar, *Grooming, Gossip, and the Evolution of Language* (Cambridge, MA: Harvard University Press, 1998).

**what psychologists refer to as "sympathy groups."** Paul Adams, *Grouped: How Small Groups of Friends Are the Key to Influence on the Social Web* (Berkeley, CA: New Riders, 2012).

**My friend Dr. Emily Anhalt, a clinical psychologist.** Learn more about Dr. Emily Anhalt's work: dremilyanhalt.com

**Research by Adam Grant.** Adam Grant, *Give and Take: A Revolutionary Approach to Success* (New York: Penguin Books, 2013).

**Noble Prize–winning novelist Toni Morrison once said.** Toni Morrison interview with Pam Houston, "The Truest Eye," *O, The Oprah Magazine*, November 2003. http://www.oprah.com/omagazine/toni-morrison-talks-love/2

**women are invited to give fewer talks than men at top US universities.** Ed Young, "Women Are Invited to Give Fewer Talks Than Men at Top U.S. Universities," *The Atlantic*, December 18, 2017. https://www.theatlantic.com/science/archive/2017/12/women-are-invited-to-give-fewer-talks-than-men-at-top-us-universities/548657

**full 100 percent of women of color working in STEM fields.** Shalene Gupta, "Study: 100% of women of color in STEM experience bias," *Fortune*, January 26, 2015. https://fortune.com/2015/01/26/study-100-of-women-of-color-in-stem-experience-bias

**Compared to every dollar that men earn, women earn just eighty cents.** Anna North, "You've heard that women 80 cents to the men's dollar. It's much worse than that," *Vox*, April 2, 2019. https://www.vox.com/policy-and-politics/2018/11/28/18116388/equal-pay-day-2019-gender-gap-equity

**As Lynne Twist, cofounder of the Pachamama Alliance.** OWN, "Lynne Twist: "What You Appreciate Appreciates," SuperSoul Sunday, Oprah Winfrey Network," YouTube Video, April 18, 2017. https://www.youtube.com/watch?v=22Z7nlnnKNE

**Aminatou and Ann even decided to go to couples therapy together.** Kara Swisher, "Aminatou Sow: Friendships matter, especially right now," Recode Decode with Kara Swisher, Podcast, June 24, 2020.

**the English poet David Whyte reminds us.** Maria Popova, "David Whyte on the True Meaning of Friendship, Love, and Heartbreak," *Brain Pickings*, April 29, 2015. https://www.brainpickings.org/2015/04/29/david-whyte-consolations-words

**You're Going to Die was started by Ned Buskirk in 2009.** Annie Vainshtein, "'You're Going to Die': Art and performance put focus on death at live shows," *SF Gate*, April 22, 2017. https://www.sfgate.com/entertainment/article/You-re-Going-to-Die-Art-and-performance-11950993.php

**Ned shared at a You're Going to Die event.** You're Going to Die website: yg2d.com. "Ned Buskirk—Live in Death's Face," Video by Danny Baldonado, uploaded August 22, 2012. https://vimeo.com/48010791

## PART FOUR: STAY IN TOUCH

***When We Rise* by Cleve Jones.** Cleve Jones, *When We Rise: My Life in the Movement* (New York: Hachette Books, 2016).

**journalist Johann Hari cites the work of John Cacioppo.** Matt D'Avella, "The Loneliness Epidemic," Interview with Johann Hari, YouTube Video, April 23, 2019. https://www.youtube.com/watch?v=m3aIQuMWJCA

**social media has contributed to society's increased polarization.** For an in-depth discussion of this topic, I recommend this article by Jonathan Haidt and Tobias Rose-Stockwell, "The Dark Psychology of Social Networks," *The Atlantic*, December 2019. https://www.theatlantic.com/magazine/archive/2019/12/social-media-democracy/600763

**A 2017 study by the Pew Research Center showed that posts exhibiting "indignant disagreement."** Pew Research Center, "Critical posts get more likes, comments, and shares than other posts," Pew Research Center, February 21, 2017. https://www.pewresearch.org/politics/2017/02/23/partisan-conflict-and-congressional-outreach/pdl-02-23-17_antipathy-new-00-02

**Another study by William J. Brady and his colleagues at NYU.** William J. Brady, Julian A. Wills, John T. Jost, Joshua A. Tucker, and Jay J. Van Bavel, "Emotion shapes the diffusion of moralized content in social networks," *PNAS*, July 11, 2017. https://www.pnas.org/content/114/28/7313

**"At most in-person events, attendees connect at a lunch break, . . . " writes connection expert Jenny Sauer-Klein.** Jenny Sauer-Klein, "3 Keys to Creating Connection at Virtual Events," *Splash*, June 11, 2020. https://splashthat.com/blog/virtual-event-connection

**Kat [Vellos] began hosting a Connection Club— "a nerdy, loving club . . ."** Learn more about Connection Club and Kat Vellos's work: weshouldgettogether.com

**Lucy Bellwood started an experimental voicemail box during quarantine called the Right Number.** Learn more Lucy Bellwood's work: lucybellwood.com

**A Few Apps That Help You Connect with Friends.** For a comprehensive look at the social wellness landscape and tech that promotes meaningful connection, here's a great article by Kasley Killam on Medium: https://medium.com/@KasleyKillam/the-growing-social-wellness-landscape-ea8f8fd11895

**"Eventually, the isolation ends," [Liz] said. "I feel better, and when I venture outside . . ."** Liz Travis Allen, "Liz Travis Allen: Getting in and out of Quarantine," *KQED*, May 5, 2020. https://www.kqed.org/perspectives/201601139844/liz-travis-allen-getting-in-and-out-of-quarantine

## PART FIVE: EMBRACE RITUAL

**regular practice of expressing gratitude changes the structure of the brain.** Madhuleena Roy Chowdhury, "The Neuroscience of Gratitude and How it Affects Anxiety and Grief," *Positive Psychology*, December 5, 2020. https://positivepsychology.com/neuroscience-of-gratitude

**Joseph Gordon-Levitt says, "If your creativity is driven by a desire to get attention . . ."** Joseph Gordon-Levitt, "How craving attention makes you less creative," TED Video, TED2019, April 2019. https://www.ted.com/talks/joseph_gordon_levitt_how_craving_attention_makes_you_less_creative

**Ethan Hawke put it beautifully when he said, "[Creativity] is vital . . ."** Ethan Hawke, "Give yourself permission to be creative," TED Video, TED2020, June 2020. https://www.ted.com/talks/ethan_hawke_give_yourself_permission_to_be_creative?language=en

**"What makes a Tea With Strangers conversation meaningful isn't that you just talked with strangers . . . "** Ankit Shah, "Being Alone," Ankit Shah website, February 2020. https://www.ankit.fyi/being-alone

**In an essay titled "Being Alone," Ankit writes.** Ibid

**this movie, like most bro comedies, normalizes rape culture.** Nina Metz, "How teen comedies like 'Superbad' normalize sexual assault," *Chicago Tribune*, October 3, 2018. https://www.chicagotribune.com/entertainment/tv/ct-mov-comedy-portrayal-sexual-assault-tv-film-1005-story.html

**In Britain, 2.5 million men admitted to having no close friends.** Melanie Hamlett, "Men Have No Friends and Women Bear the Burden," *Harper's Bazaar*, May 2, 2019. https://www.harpersbazaar.com/culture/features/a27259689/toxic-masculinity-male-friendships-emotional-labor-men-rely-on-women

**Men conceal pain and illness at much higher rates than women.** Ibid.

**Ashanti Branch has made it his life's work.** Learn more about Ashanti Branch's work and Ever Forward Club: everforwardclub.org

**Kat Vellos wrote *Connected from Afar*.** Kat Vellos, *Connected from Afar: A Guide for Staying Close When You're Far Away* (Kat Vellos, 2020).

**Mel Brooks drove from Santa Monica to Beverly Hills.** Hadley Freeman, "'Love and free food': Mel Brooks and Carl Reiner share the secrets of their 70-year friendship," *The Guardian*, February 20, 2020. https://www.theguardian.com/global/2020/feb/20/love-and-free-food-mel-brooks-and-carl-reiner-share-the-secrets-of-their-70-year-friendship

## PART SIX: BE A MINISTER FOR LONELINESS IN YOUR COMMUNITY

**young people aged sixteen to twenty-four are the most likely demographic to report feeling lonely.** Esteban Ortiz-Ospina, "Is there a loneliness epidemic?," *Our World in Data*, December 11, 2019. https://ourworldindata.org/loneliness-epidemic

**The Intergenerational Learning Center . . .** Intergenerational Learning Center website, https://washington.providence.org/services-directory/services/i/intergenerational-learning-center

**nonprofit organization Encore helps retirees.** Learn more about Encore's Gen2Gen campaign: https://generationtogeneration.org

**Cleveland Clinic estimates that as many as 50–75 percent of new mothers.** Cleveland Clinic, "Depression after the Birth of a Child or Pregnancy Loss," Cleveland Clinic website. https://my.clevelandclinic.org/health/diseases/9312-depression-after-the-birth-of-a-child-or-pregnancy-loss

**Although Zora was a highly acclaimed writer, the largest royalty [Zora Neale Hurston] ever earned.** "About Zora Neale Hurston," Zora Neale Hurston website. https://www.zoranealehurston.com/about

**Zora's House strives to embody Shine Theory . . . developed by Aminatou Sow and Ann Friedman.** Aminatou Sow and Ann Friedman, "Who created Shine Theory?," Shine Theory website. https://www.shinetheory.com/who-created-shine-theory

**Black women, who face higher maternal and infant mortality rates.** Linda Villarosa, "Why America's Black Mothers and Babies Are in a Life-or-Death Crisis," *New York Times*, April 11, 2018. https://www.nytimes.com/2018/04/11/magazine/black-mothers-babies-death-maternal-mortality.html

**that 7 percent of voters lost or ended a friendship because of the 2016 election.** Daniel Bukszpan, "Tough election leaves countless tattered online friendships in its wake," *CNBC*, November 12, 2016. https://www.cnbc.com/2016/11/11/tough-election-leaves-countless-tattered-online-friendships-in-its-wake.html

**80 percent of Americans.** Tovia Smith, "'Dude, I'm Done': When Politics Tears Families And Friendships Apart," *NPR*, October 27, 2020. https://www.npr.org/2020/10/27/928209548/dude-i-m-done-when-politics-tears-families-and-friendships-apart

**Scott and his colleague, Jason Marsh, write that there's a difference between *agreement* and *understanding*.** Scott Shigeoka and Jason Marsh, "Eight Keys to Bridging Our Differences," *Greater Good Magazine*, July 22, 2020. https://greatergood.berkeley.edu/article/item/eight_keys_to_bridging_our_differences

**Stephen R. Covey, author of *The 7 Habits of Highly Effective People*, called empathic listening.** Stephen R. Covey, "Using Empathic Listening to Collaborate," *Fast Company*, December 26, 2011. https://www.fastcompany.com/1727872/using-empathic-listening-collaborate

**the story of how Derek Black.** Terry Gross, "How a Rising Star of White Nationalism Broke Free from the Movement, *NPR*, September 24, 2018. https://www.npr.org/2018/09/24/651052970/how-a-rising-star-of-white-nationalism-broke-free-from-the-movement

**nine million people in Britain often or always feel lonely.** Ceylan Yeginsu, "U.K. Appoints a Minister for Loneliness," *New York Times*, January 17, 2018. https://www.nytimes.com/2018/01/17/world/europe/uk-britain-loneliness.html

**Ivan Cash is an award-winning interactive artist.** Learn more about Ivan's work: ivan.cash

**Ivan profiles William Cromartie, a Bay Area Rapid Transit (BART) employee.** William Cromartie in *Agent of Connection*, Vimeo Video, Directed by Ivan Cash, 2017. https://vimeo.com/238328937

**Brené Brown's words . . . "He or she who chooses comfort over courage . . . "** Krista Tippet, "Brené Brown: Strong Back, Soft Front, Wild Heart," *On Being with Krista Tippet*, February 8, 2018. https://onbeing.org/programs/brene-brown-strong-back-soft-front-wild-heart

**three-quarters of white Americans don't have any non-white friends.** Christopher Ingraham, "Three quarters of whites don't have any non-white friends," *Washington Post*, August 25, 2014. https://www.washingtonpost.com/news/wonk/wp/2014/08/25/three-quarters-of-whites-dont-have-any-non-white-friends/

**French sociologist Émile Dirkheim called this experience "collective effervescence,"** Krista Tippet, "Brené Brown: Strong Back, Soft Front, Wild Heart," *On Being with Krista Tippet*, January 2, 2020. https://onbe-ing.org/programs/brene-brown-strong-back-soft-front-wild-heart

**In their seminal report about the future of community building called *How We Gather*, Angie Thurston and Casper ter Kuile.** Angie Thurston and Casper ter Kuile, "How We Gather," Sacred Design Lab, April 2015. https://sacred.design/wp-content/uploads/2019/10/How_We_Gather_Digital_4.11.17.pdf

**follow in the footsteps of four couples that have been best friends for twenty years.** Kelly McLaughlin, "Welcome to 'Bestie Row'! Friends build an entire community of tiny houses next to each other so they can live as neighbors," *Daily Mail*, May 11, 2015. https://www.dailymail.co.uk/news/article-3077686/Llano-Exit-Strategy-brings-eight-friends-row-tiny-houses-neighbors.html

**Here's what Levi posted.** Levi Felix, Facebook post, July 29, 2016. https://www.facebook.com/levifelix/posts/10104773226827007

# About the Author

.....................

**Adam Smiley Poswolsky** is a millennial workplace expert, motivational speaker, and author of *The Quarter-Life Breakthrough* and *The Breakthrough Speaker*.

Smiley helps companies attract, retain, and empower the next generation, and he has inspired thousands of professionals to be more engaged at work, through speaking at companies like Google, Apple, Facebook, Unilever, Deloitte, and Stanford University Graduate School of Business. Smiley's TEDx talk on "the quarter-life crisis" has been viewed more than 1.5 million times, and he has spoken in front of fifty thousand people in twenty countries. Smiley has advised heads of state and foreign leaders about millennials, multigenerational engagement, and fostering connection and belonging in the digital age.

Smiley's work has been featured in the *New Yorker*, the *New York Times*, the *Washington Post*, *Fast Company*, CNN, and the World Economic Forum, among many other outlets. Smiley is a thirteen-time camp counselor at Camp Grounded: Summer Camp for Adults and advisory board member for Digital Detox.

In 2017, Smiley launched the Women/Womxn, BIPOC and Inclusivity Speaker Initiative, a community that aims to increase the number of women and people of color speaking at conferences and companies, as well as ensure that women and other underrepresented speakers are paid competitively as compared to their colleagues. The group now has more than four thousand members.

Smiley is a proud graduate of Wesleyan University and can usually be found dancing in the San Francisco Bay Area.

SMILEYPOSWOLSKY.COM
SMILEYPOSWOLSKY.COM/FRIENDSHIP
@WHATSUPSMILEY

Smiley is available for speaking
engagements. To inquire, please visit
smileyposwolsky.com/speaking